Cambridge Elements ☰

Elements in the Philosophy of Religion
edited by
Yujin Nagasawa
University of Birmingham

THE INCARNATION

Timothy J. Pawl
University of St. Thomas

CAMBRIDGE
UNIVERSITY PRESS

CAMBRIDGE
UNIVERSITY PRESS

University Printing House, Cambridge CB2 8BS, United Kingdom

One Liberty Plaza, 20th Floor, New York, NY 10006, USA

477 Williamstown Road, Port Melbourne, VIC 3207, Australia

314–321, 3rd Floor, Plot 3, Splendor Forum, Jasola District Centre,
New Delhi – 110025, India

79 Anson Road, #06–04/06, Singapore 079906

Cambridge University Press is part of the University of Cambridge.

It furthers the University's mission by disseminating knowledge in the pursuit of
education, learning, and research at the highest international levels of excellence.

www.cambridge.org
Information on this title: www.cambridge.org/9781108457521
DOI: 10.1017/9781108558341

First published 2020

Nihil Obstat	*Imprimatur*
Reverend George Welzbacher	The Most Reverend Bernard Hebda
Censor Librorum	Archbishop of Saint Paul and Minneapolis
November 5, 2019	November 5, 2019

The *Nihil Obstat* and *Imprimatur* are official declarations that a book is free of doctrinal
error. No implication is contained therein that those who have granted the *Nihil
Obstat* and *Imprimatur* agree with the content, opinions, or statements expressed. Nor
do they assume any legal responsibility associated with publication.

A catalogue record for this publication is available from the British Library.

ISBN 978-1-108-45752-1 Paperback
ISSN 2399-5165 (online)
ISSN 2515-9763 (print)

The Incarnation

Elements in the Philosophy of Religion

DOI: 10.1017/9781108558341
First published online: September 2020

Timothy J. Pawl
University of St. Thomas

Author for correspondence: Timothy J. Pawl, timpawl@stthomas.edu

Abstract: The doctrine of the Incarnation, that Jesus Christ was both truly God and truly human, is the foundation and cornerstone of traditional Christian theism. And yet this traditional teaching appears to verge on incoherence. How can one person be both God, having all the perfections of divinity, and human, having all the limitations of humanity? This is the fundamental philosophical problem of the Incarnation. Perhaps a solution is found in an analysis of what the traditional teaching meant by *person*, *divinity*, and *humanity*, or in understanding how divinity and humanity were *united* in a single person. This Element presents that traditional teaching, then returns to the incoherence problem to showcase various solutions offered to it.

Keywords: Incarnation, Conciliar Christology, theism, metaphysics

ISBNs: 9781108457521 (PB), 9781108558341 (OC)
ISSNs: 2399–5165 (online), 2515–9763 (print)

Contents

1 Introduction

The doctrine of the Incarnation is the teaching that Jesus Christ, the human crucified under Pontius Pilate, was truly God, one person of the Blessed Trinity. That doctrine, affirmed by the orthodox statements of faith from the early church through the later Catholic, Orthodox, and Protestant doctrinal statements, teaches that this person, while truly God, became truly human, a human like other humans in all ways except sin, for the sake of saving humans from their sins and bringing them to perfect union with God. This doctrine is a fundamental part of any traditional Christian teaching – if it is false, so is traditional Christianity.

While we may have become accustomed to it, the doctrine of the Incarnation is a shocking claim. How could God become human? How could one person be two seemingly incompatible types of things at the same time? If God is conceptualized in the traditional sense as immutable, impassible, and simple, how could such a person *become* changeable, affectable, and complex, as all humans are? And *why*? Why would God do such a thing as to become human?

1.1 Methodology

The Incarnation has been analyzed from multiple perspectives. For instance, do the Christian Scriptures imply that Jesus is true God, one in being with the Father?[1] Does the historical record give justification for belief in the existence of the flesh-and-blood human named "Jesus," son of Mary? Do the early theologians affirm the doctrine? And so on. All of these scriptural and historical questions are worthy of analysis. This short Element, situated as it is in a series on the philosophy of religion, does not address these questions. Rather, it focuses on the *philosophical* questions surrounding the doctrine. Such philosophical analysis no doubt assumes some findings of these other methods of assessment. For instance, it assumes, for the sake of argument, that the human, Jesus, did exist.[2] But it does not and could not, given length constraints, responsibly enter into the other discussions.

While this Element focuses exclusively on the philosophical questions concerning the Incarnation, its work cannot be done in a historical vacuum. The doctrine of the Incarnation was formulated in a series of ecumenical councils – the context of the statements of those councils must be taken into account to understand the meaning they had for those speakers. This Element makes

---

[1] The biblical justification for the doctrine of the Incarnation is vitally important. This Element is not the place to enter into that vast literature. It is impossible to provide a brief set of paradigmatic references to the ocean of literature on the biblical case for the doctrine of the Incarnation. I suggest the reader start with Bird et al. (2014), Loke (2019), and Tilling (2015) and follow the footnotes into the wider literature.

[2] For scholarship on the historical case for the existence of Jesus, see Ehrman (2013).

frequent reference to the doctrinal statements of these councils concerning the Incarnation.

Many of the philosophers who have considered the philosophical questions concerning the Incarnation have done so from a specific heritage. For instance, many who believe in the Incarnation would be reluctant to affirm something that contradicts the teachings of the ecumenical Council of Chalcedon in AD 451. Likewise, many who object to the Incarnation want their objections to target the traditional teaching and would see it as a misfire if their objections showed that a view of the Incarnation not held by anyone in Christian history is incoherent. For this reason, this Element notes whether a certain line of philosophical thought is precluded by the orthodox statements concerning the Incarnation. Throughout I make use of the excellent translation edited by Norman Tanner (1990), *Decrees of the Ecumenical Councils*. In the hopes of providing some evidence that I have not interpreted these texts in a nontraditional manner, I have sought out and received a *Nihil Obstat* and *Imprimatur* on this Element from my local Catholic diocese, the Diocese of Saint Paul and Minneapolis.

A note on language: the word "orthodox" is often used as a term of praise, and its contrary, "nonorthodox" or "heretical," is often used as a term of derision. In this work, "orthodox" is stripped of such resonance, and I make no use of "heretical" at all. (Here I've *mentioned* it twice.[3]) As I use the term, orthodox teaching is that which is endorsed in the earliest seven ecumenical councils, and a proposition is "nonorthodox" when it is proscribed by those same councils. The reader will see that these definitions leave a large middle ground: things neither taught nor proscribed by those councils, for instance, the claim that Christ knew English. There is debate about what ought to count as orthodox. I have no room here to enter into that debate. I stipulate instead a meaning that I think finds consensus throughout the history of Christian thought.

This Element presents the Christology promulgated by the first seven ecumenical councils of Christianity: the First Council of Nicaea in 325, the First Council of Constantinople in 381, the Council of Ephesus in 431, the Council of Chalcedon in 451, the Second Council of Constantinople in 553, the Third Council of Constantinople in 680–681, and the Second Council of Nicaea in 787. I refer to the Christology of these councils as *Conciliar Christology*.

A final point about method: this Element speaks in a factive voice, as if the Incarnation in fact occurred. Appending "according to Conciliar Christology" or the like to each sentence would be tiresome for both author and reader. The reader who does not affirm the Incarnation and who finds such factive

---

[3] For helpful reflection on the concepts of "orthodoxy" and "heresy," see Stump (1999).

presentation unpalatable ought to treat the remainder of this Element as resting on an assumption made for the sake of argument. Assume that the world is as the Christians have believed, and that there was an Incarnation. In fact, we don't even need so strong an assumption. We can simply assume the *possible truth* of the doctrine and still let this Element do its work.

1.2 What the Doctrine of the Incarnation Says

The teachings of Conciliar Christology can be organized under five topical headings: the person of Christ, the divine nature of Christ, the human nature of Christ, the union between the two natures (i.e., the *hypostatic* union), and the activities of the God-man, Jesus Christ. In this Introduction, I offer an initial comment about conciliar teaching on these five topics.

To the first point: Jesus Christ is one person, the Second Person of the Trinity, referred to also as "the Son" and "the Word." There are not two persons in the Incarnation, one divine and the other human. Rather, there is one person who is both truly divine and truly human because this one person had and has two distinct natures.

To the second point: one of those natures was the one and only divine nature, which Jesus possessed with and no less than the Father and the Holy Spirit. God the Son made human, Jesus, was immutable and impassible in virtue of the divine nature. His incarnation in no sense diminished his possession of that divine nature.

To the third point: the other nature was a human nature that the Son took up into himself in the Incarnation (the technical term is *assumed*). In virtue of this human nature Christ was like us in all ways, sin alone excluded.

To the fourth point: these two natures were united in a unique manner. This union is traditionally referred to as the *hypostatic union*. It is *hypostatic*, insofar as the union occurs in the person of the Son, and *person*, as we see in Section 2.2, is a species of the genus, *hypostasis*. It is this hypostatic union between the natures that allows for the Communication of Idioms (*Communicatio Idiomatum*), the true description of the one person using a subject term drawn from one nature and a predicate term drawn from another. To give a common example, Paul says in 1 Corinthians 2:8 that the leaders of the world crucified the Lord of glory. Here the "Lord of glory" (a term correct of Christ in virtue of his divinity) is "crucified" (a term correct of Christ in virtue of his humanity).

To the fifth point: Christ died, rose from the dead, and ascended into heaven. He willed. He knew. Many questions arise from such observations. How can it be that God dies? Did he will evil? *Could* he have willed evil? Could he have been tempted? Could he have been mistaken?

1.3 The Main Metaphysical Problem

Predicating terms of one and the same person drawn from two different natures leads to difficulties, as the councils themselves make evident. The traditional documents of Christianity assert both classical theistic attributes of Christ (e.g., impassible, immutable) and also mundane human attributes (e.g., suffered, changed). Sometimes, as we see in Section 7.1, they predicate both apparently contradictory predicates of Christ in the very same sentence!

It is these apparent contradictions in attributes that lead to what has been called the Fundamental Philosophical Problem of the Incarnation (see Cross 2011, 453). How could one person be both God and human? For to be truly God, that person would have to be eternal, omnipotent, omniscient, immutable, impassible, and all the rest. But to be truly human, that person would have to be temporal, weak in some ways, ignorant of some facts, able to change, able to be affected, and so on. And nothing can be both eternal and temporal, or omnipotent and weak, or … And so nothing can be both God and human. Thus, Christ is not both God and human, and so the doctrine of the Incarnation is false.

The Fundamental Philosophical Problem is the most important philosophical objection to the doctrine of the Incarnation. But to answer an objection to a doctrine properly, one must know what the doctrine says, which is why this objection comes at the end of this Element, after explaining the doctrine.[4]

1.4 The Shape of Things to Come

This Element is composed of eight sections. The Introduction, now concluding, discusses the methods I employ and offers some caveats. For instance, the method is analytic, with attention paid to the traditional formulations of the doctrine. The caveats include the claim that this Element does not assess biblical or historical evidence for or against the doctrine.

Section 2, on the person of Christ, addresses the definitions of the key terms, "hypostasis" and "person," the names of the person (e.g., Logos, Son), and the divine status of the person. Section 3, on the divinity of Christ, discusses the divine nature and its attributes from two perspectives: the traditional view and the kenotic view. Section 4, on the humanity of Christ, considers human nature itself, whether it is concrete or abstract, whether it is composed of parts and if so how many, whether it has a will and a mind, whether it is a person in its own

---

[4] This Element focuses on the metaphysics of the Incarnation. Those interested in the atoning work of the Incarnation should see Stump (2019) and, in this same Elements series, Craig (2018). For discussion of epistemic questions concerning the acceptance of doctrine, including the Incarnation, see McNabb (2018) from this same Elements series.

right, whether it is fallen or unfallen, and the weaknesses or infirmities it has. Section 5, on the hypostatic union, discusses whether the union can be fully analyzed philosophically, what features it has of itself (e.g., is it created?), and what we can say of the Communication of Idioms from the natures to the person, in light of the union. Section 6 focuses on the activities of Christ, including his will (Was it free? Could he sin?), his knowledge (Was he mistaken?), his death, and his descent into hell. Section 7 discusses the main philosophical objection, which is that anything divine must have certain predications true of it, but nothing human can have those predications true of it; thus, Christ couldn't be both divine and human, contrary to the orthodox doctrine. The last section is both more complex and longer than the previous sections, insofar as it takes up many of the extant responses to the problem, some of which are quite technical.

2 The Person

The traditional doctrine of the Trinity teaches both that there is only one God and that there are three divine persons: the Father, the Son, and the Holy Spirit. Only one of these three persons, the Son, became incarnate. This Element focuses exclusively on the Second Person of the Trinity, the one who, according to Scripture and council, became human.

The focus on this person should begin at the outset with a discussion concerning the term "person." Once the traditional meaning of that term is clarified, I discuss the terms used to name that person, as confusion on those terms can spell havoc for our conceptual clarity in these discussions.

2.1 The Definitions of the Terms "Hypostasis" and "Person"

Jesus Christ is referred to as both a person and a hypostasis in the conciliar texts. To give just one example, as Cyril says in his third letter to Nestorius, accepted at the Council of Ephesus,

> Why should he who submitted himself to voluntary self-emptying for our sake, reject expressions that are suitable for such self-emptying? All the expressions, therefore, that occur in the gospels are to be referred to one person, the one enfleshed hypostasis of the Word. For there is one Lord Jesus Christ, according to the scriptures. (Tanner 1990, 56)

What, though, is meant by these terms, "hypostasis" and "person," such that Christ counts as exactly one hypostasis and exactly one person?

Elsewhere (Pawl 2016d, 32), I have followed the work of Marilyn McCord Adams (2005, 37) and Alfred Freddoso (1986, 49) in analyzing the term "hypostasis" (in the Latin translation, "supposit"), following the Medievals, to mean:

Supposit (Hypostasis)	X is a supposit (hypostasis) if and only if x is a complete being, incommunicable by identity, not apt to inhere in anything, and not sustained by anything.

The first clause of the right side of the biconditional is intended to preclude parts of supposits from being supposits themselves – my hand is not itself a supposit, to use Aquinas's example (*ST* III q.16 a.12 ad.2).[5] Wholes, not parts of wholes, are supposits. The second clause is included for technical Trinitarian reasons. In brief, the question arose whether the divine nature itself is a hypostasis, in addition to the three divine persons. The answer had to be "no" for traditional Christianity, since there are only three, not four, persons. This second clause is meant to safeguard that "no" answer. To be communicable by identity is for the very same thing to be both had by one thing and given to another without the former ceasing to have it. Things that are communicable in such a manner aren't themselves supposits. The third clause is meant to preclude anything accidental from counting as a hypostasis. This was a worry, since some views of the Eucharist claim that accidental forms could exist without inhering in substances.[6] Such non-inhering accidents are not supposits in their own right. The fourth is most relevant to our purposes. The Medievals intended the notion of being "sustained" here to preclude the human nature of Christ, which is sustained *by* the person, from itself counting as a hypostasis.[7] That human nature exists *in* the Word, depending on the Word for its existence. Things that depend upon others in the way that the human nature depends upon the person are not supposits in their own right.[8] One can find similar understandings of hypostasis throughout the Christian tradition.[9]

With this notion of hypostasis in hand, forming a notion of personhood is an easy matter. A person, on the traditional understanding of the term, is a hypostasis that has a rational nature.[10] All supposits have some nature or other. Dogs have their own natures, slugs have their own, humans have their

---

[5] This citation ought to be read: Aquinas's *Summa Theologica*, third part, question 16, article 12, response to objection 2.

[6] For discussion of this point, see Pawl (2012).

[7] See also de Aldama and Solano (2014, 42–53) on this point.

[8] It is true that, in another sense, everything created is sustained in existence by God on the traditional Christian view. That is a different sense of the term "sustained." The Medievals were not saying that nothing created is a supposit.

[9] See, for instance, Carlson (2012, 129, 259), Geddes (1911), Gorman (2000b; 2017, chap. 1), John of Damascus (1958, 20, 56), Pohle (1911, 222), Rebenich (2002, 73), Salano and de Aldama (2014, 42–43), and Tanner (2001, 32).

[10] To see other discussions of this traditional conception of "person", see Adams (2005, 23–24), Aquinas (2012, 13), Carlson (2012, 204), Cupitt (1977, 135), Ferrier (1962, 81), Flint (2012, 189), Geddes (1911), Gorman (2011, 430), Lonergan (2016, 387–389), Pawl (2016d, 32–33; 2019b, 22), Pohle (1911, 224), Sturch (1991, 269–274), Turcescu (2005), Twombly (2015, 57–60), Wesche (1997, 95, 126), and C.J.F. Williams (1968, 517).

own, etc. But only some of those natures are rational. And so only some supposits count as persons.

Interestingly and importantly, the notion of person used in these discussions is not a modern notion of personhood, called by some in the debate a Lockean notion of personhood (Cf. Pohle 1911, 226). Such a notion has it that personhood is, as Carlson (2012, 204) defines it, "An individual who manifests the developed traits and abilities associated with human, personal life (e.g. self-awareness, deliberate choice and action)." The reason this modern definition will be insufficient for the Christological (and Trinitarian) contexts becomes more explicit in the discussion of the humanity of Christ in Section 4. In brief, though, the traditional view is that Christ had a human element – a body/soul composite – that some argue fulfilled the conditions for being a person *in this modern sense of the term*. This may lead some to believe that there are two persons – "persons" in the sense relevant to the doctrine – in the Incarnation, something the conciliar texts and traditional Christian orthodoxy adamantly deny. This is just one example of how ignorance of the historical meaning of the technical terms can cause confusion concerning the traditional doctrine. In Section 2.3, we see another instance of confusion over terms.

2.2 One Person of the Trinity

Jesus Christ is a person – a hypostasis of a rational nature. Not only that, he is one person of the Blessed Trinity on the orthodox Christian view. Third Constantinople says as much, claiming that the council, along with the previous five councils, "professes our lord Jesus Christ our true God, one of the holy Trinity" (Tanner 1990, 127). This person did not come into existence within the Virgin Mary (a view Cyril calls "absurd and stupid" in the conciliar texts [Tanner 1990, 42]). Rather, this person "existed before every age and is coeternal with the Father" (Tanner 1990, 42). Since he is a member of the Trinity, coeternal with the Father, he is a divine person.

Is Jesus a human person, as well as a divine person? This question has typically been answered in the negative throughout Christian history, for complicated reasons. Such an answer has caused confusion in some thinkers. For it seems that one rightly counts as a human person if one is both human and a person. Christ fulfills both criteria. Christ "became human" according to the Nicene Creed. Moreover, as we've seen, he is a person. Why, then, this denial of Christ's being a human person? We can see the hesitancy here by looking at the history of the term "human person" in the Christological discourse, combined with a traditional prudential maxim from those debates.

Concerning the history, the term "human person" was used to mean *merely* human person. As such, speaking in this way was viewed as problematic by orthodox proponents of the Incarnation. Philosophers will rightly note that "human person" doesn't logically entail "merely human person" by itself. But philosophers will do well to remember that, in matters of preaching and teaching, *conversational* implicature is at least as important as logical implicature.

Concerning the traditional prudential maxim from Christological debates, the idea was not to speak as the opponents spoke, for fear of leading astray the laity. Aquinas, for instance, notes that while it is true that Christ is impassible in his divine nature, one ought not to say so unqualifiedly, as it may appear to be a word in favor of the view of the Manicheans, who thought that Christ had no real body (*ST* III q.16 a.8 ad.2). The same prudential maxim would lead the orthodox proponents of the Incarnation not to speak in ways that appear to support the view of the Arians, who thought Christ was not a divine person in the same sense the Father is. To make explicit that they were affirming neither a Manichean nor an Arian view of Christ, some thinkers in the tradition took to calling Christ a "Theandric" person. The English word "theandric" comes from two Greek roots, which in the nominative are *theos*, for God, and *anēr*, for man (which is *andros* in the genitive case).[11]

2.3 The Names of the Person

Many terms are used in the Christological writings: "Jesus," "the Christ," "the Word," "the Son," "the Logos," "the Second Person of the Trinity," etc. There is some disagreement about what exactly is referred to with each term. We can see this most clearly if we focus on the name "Jesus Christ."

Some people use "Jesus Christ" to refer to the assumed human nature alone (cf. Holland 2012, 81; Marmodoro and Hill 2011, 13; and Sturch 1991, 122, 141).[12] Others use "Jesus Christ" to refer to the person of the Son, the very person that exists eternally with the Father and Holy Spirit, and who assumes human flesh from Mary (cf. Alfeyev 2012, 265; Pawl 2016d, 46–47; Jedwab 2011, 169; Rea 2011, 150; and Wesche 1997, 12–13). Finally, some use that name to refer to a third thing, not the assumed human nature alone, and not the person of the Son or the Word. Rather, they use the name "Jesus Christ" to refer to a compound – in some sense of compound – of that person and the human nature into a "larger" entity.[13] The view here is that "Jesus Christ" names

---

[11] I thank Jonathan Rutledge for discussion of the Greek roots here.

[12] In doing so, they are understanding the nature in the concrete sense discussed later in Section 4.1.2.

[13] See Crisp (2011; 2016, chap. 6), Leftow (2011, 321), and Turner (2019, n. 5).

a contingent entity, not itself a person, but that has a person as a part (see section 5.3 for more on this view, there called "Model A").

In this Element, I use the terms "Jesus Christ," "Word," "Second Person," "the Son," and all the rest as co-referring personal terms. They refer, in my usage, to one and the same person. I have argued for this usage of the terms elsewhere on conciliar grounds (Pawl 2016d, 46–47), grounds Flint (2011, 81n.17) shares. Against the first view, that "Jesus" names the human nature alone, we do well to recall that the councils call Jesus "true God" and "one of the Holy Trinity" (Tanner 1990, 127). No human nature, though, is one of the Holy Trinity or truly God. Against both the first and third views, the councils call Jesus a hypostasis and a person, as we saw in Section 2.2. The Word too, though, is a person. If we look back to the truth conditions for being a hypostasis in Section 2.1, we see that no hypostasis can have a distinct hypostasis as a component, since each hypostasis is a complete being in its own right. And so the Word and Jesus cannot be related to one another as component to whole, since they are both referred to by "person" and "hypostasis." There must be two distinct persons, then, or the names must refer to the very same thing. If distinct persons, we have a nonorthodox view sometimes labeled "Nestorianism." If the terms co-refer, then the naming convention I use in this Element is the correct one.[14]

It is true that the name "Jesus Christ" is bound up with the Incarnation, such that had the Word not become incarnate, he wouldn't have had that name. Presumably, "the Second Person" is not contingent upon the Incarnation in the same sense. Even so, that doesn't show that the two terms do not co-refer.

2.4 Conclusion

In summary, the Word, the Son, the Second Person of the Trinity, is a person – a hypostasis of a rational nature. That very person became human and is the one and only divine person to have become incarnate.[15] As I use the term in this Element, "Jesus Christ" is the name of a person, and that person is the very same person as the Word.

---

[14] See Section 5.3 for more discussion of the relation between Jesus and the Word.

[15] It is an interesting question whether the other two divine persons *could* have become incarnate. For more on that question, see Adams (1985; 2005; 2006, 198–199; 2009, 241;), de Aldama and Solano (2014, 63), Aquinas (*ST* III q.3), Arendzen (1941, 161), Baker (2013, 47), Bonting (2003), Brazier (2013), Craig (2006, 63), Crisp (2008; 2009, chap. 8), Cross (2005, 230–232), Cuff (2015, 366–371), Davies (2003), Fisher and Fergusson (2006), Flint (2001, 312; 2012, 192–198), Freddoso (1983; 1986), George (2001), Gondreau (2018, 145–150), Gorman (2016), Hebblethwaite (2001; 2008, 74), Jaeger (2017), Kereszty (2002, 382), Kevern (2002), Le Poidevin (2009a, 183; 2011), Mascall (1965, 40–41), Morris (1987, 183), O'Collins (2002, 19–23), Pawl (2016a; 2016c; 2019b, chaps. 2 and 3), Pohle (1913, 136), Schmaus (1971, 241–242), Sturch (1991, 43, 194–200), and Ward (1998, 162).

3 The Divinity of Christ

The previous section discussed the person of Christ. This section is the first of two that take up the question of *what* Christ is: fully God and fully human. This section focuses on his divinity, whereas the next section focuses on his humanity.

3.1 The Divine Nature Itself

According to traditional Christian teaching, there is only one divine nature, also referred to as the divine substance or the divine essence (Tanner 1990, 114). That one divine nature is possessed (in some sense) by the three divine persons. The claim that there is only one divine nature is intended to protect against tritheism; the distinction between the three persons is intended to protect against modalism (the view that the Father, Son, and Spirit are merely different ways that the one divine person chooses to manifest himself to the world).[16]

3.2 The Attributes of the Divine Nature

Scholars have presented various views concerning the attributes of the divine nature. This section canvasses the main views in the contemporary debate.

3.2.1 The Classical View

On one understanding, the divine nature has the attributes of classical theism. On this theory, the nature is impassible and so unable to be causally affected. The nature is immutable and so unable to change. It is atemporal and so outside of time. And it is simple so without any ontological complexity.[17]

Parts of this view receive support from the conciliar texts.[17] For instance, concerning immutability, the Council of Ephesus teaches that Christ "is unchangeable and immutable by nature" (Tanner 1990, 51). The same council teaches that "those are quite mad who suppose that 'a shadow of change' is conceivable in connexion with the divine nature of the Word" (Tanner 1990, 72). Concerning impassibility, Chalcedon says that it is an error to claim that "the divine nature of the Only-begotten is passible" (Tanner 1990, 84). Moreover, Chalcedon "expels from the assembly of the priests those who dare to say that the divinity of the Only-begotten is passible" (85–86).

Evidence for atemporality in the councils is less clear. Leo writes in his *Tome to Flavian*, part of the accepted documents from Chalcedon, that "whilst

---

[16] See Hasker (2019) for a recent discussion of the divine nature.

[17] To see the conciliar evidence in much greater detail, as well as evidence from later Catholic, Orthodox, and Protestant sources, see Pawl (2016d, chaps. 8, Section II).

remaining pre-existent, [the Son of God] begins to exist in time [*ante tempora manens esse coepit ex tempore*]" (Tanner 1990, 79). The Second Council of Constantinople includes an anathema that declares accursed those who will not say that the Son has a nativity from the Father *achronos*, that is, outside time. Neither of these texts proves that the divine *nature* is atemporal. But they do give some reason to think that the Son is atemporal, and he clearly is not atemporal due to his human nature. So there is reason to think that it is due to his divinity itself that he is atemporal. Concerning simplicity, there is no explicit affirmation from the first seven councils that the divine nature is simple. Later councils and confessional statements, though, Catholic, Orthodox, and Protestant, include the divinity's simplicity as a teaching.[18]

3.2.2 Nonclassical Views

There are various ways one might understand the divine nature such that it doesn't have the robust attributes classical theism ascribes to it. One standard term for the most-attested contemporary school of thought concerning the divine nature that is contrary to classical theism is "theistic personalism." I avoid that term here, primarily because the rivalry between these two approaches to God spills out into other topics besides the divine nature, for instance, how God creates and whether God is a person or merely personal.[19] Those topics aren't germane to the purposes of this Element and so would be an unnecessary rabbit trail to follow.

Another theory that may appear relevant here is kenotic Christology, which is the topic of Section 7.3.4. Briefly, kenotic Christology claims that Christ emptied himself of some of his divine attributes when he became incarnate. For instance, he went from being omniscient to being limited in knowledge, or omnipresent to being located only at a certain place. Such a view has an oblique relation to the theory of the divine nature, for such a view requires that omniscience is not an essential feature of divinity. Were it essential, Christ would cease being divine when he lacks knowledge during the Incarnation. Thomas Morris draws out the implications for divinity explicitly when he notes that to be divine, on the kenotic view, wouldn't require omniscience, but rather omniscience-unless-incarnate.[20] Likewise for other attributes that cause

---

[18] For examples, see the Catholic Fourth Lateran Council (Tanner 1990, 230–232), the first three decrees of the Orthodox Third Hesychastic Council, and the Reformed Belgic Confession of Faith, Article 1.

[19] For a discussion of the distinction between classical theism and theistic personalism, and to see where the latter term was coined, see B. Davies (2004, chap. 1). For more on whether God is a person or personal, see Page (2019)

[20] See Morris (1987, 99); see also Forrest (2009, 130–131).

Incarnational worries – they all get an "unless" modification. Even still, one might think that the divine nature itself has the attributes of classical theism, even if the persons can freely choose to be empty of those attributes, and so kenotic Christology does not imply that the divine nature itself is not simple, atemporal, immutable, and impassible.[21]

The main alternatives to classical theism seldom reject the listed attributes wholesale. For instance, many keep the language of divine eternity, but understand eternity as implying everlastingness, and not atemporality.[22] Or one might deny that God is unchanging *metaphysically* speaking, but retain that God is unchanging *morally* speaking.[23] Likewise, God might be causally affectable, but unable to be caused to suffer psychologically.

These are common alternatives in the philosophical discussion of the Incarnation. They do not, though, sit easily with the conciliar texts. If Christ was already existing in time everlastingly, in what sense could he go from being preexistent to beginning to exist in time, as we saw Chalcedon teach in Section 3.2.1? Moreover, we can tell the sense the councils give to the attributes by seeing the work they intend the attributes to do. They use immutability, for instance, to preclude ontological change in the divine nature, not merely to point out moral constancy (Tanner 1990, 51).[24]

3.3 A Comparison of the Conceptions of Divinity with Respect to the Incarnation

Depending on one's conception of the divine attributes, the philosophical problems that arise from the Incarnation will be different. To see how, consider the philosophical objection that is the focus of Section 7.

Section 7 focuses on the objection that nothing can be both God and human, since to be God it would have to be a way that no human could be. If one denies that God is as the classical conception requires, then one needn't answer the question of how Christ was both, say, impassible and passible during the Incarnation. Generally speaking, the problem of Section 7 can be viewed as a "metaphysical size-gap," as Marilyn McCord Adams termed it (2000, 103; 2004). The more one shrinks that gap by denying classical attributes of God, the fewer problems one will have with rendering the Incarnation coherent.

---

[21] Such a view would hold that while the self-emptying of the person requires change *in the person*, it doesn't require change *in the divine nature*. I leave the spelling out of the mechanics of such a view to its proponents.

[22] See Deng (2018) and Mullins (2016).   [23] See Dorner (1994) and Swinburne (1993, 219).

[24] For a much fuller discussion of the use of immutability in the conciliar texts, see Pawl (2016d, 107–114).

3.4 Conclusion

This section explicated various views of the attributes of the divine nature. According to Conciliar Christology, that nature is immutable and impassible. A case could be made for its atemporality from those texts too, but such is not explicit, as are impassibility and immutability. The section also discussed how the rival conceptions of divinity affect the problems that face a philosophy of the Incarnation.

4 The Humanity of Christ

The account of Christ's humanity is vexed in the contemporary philosophical discussion. Is it something abstract, like a shareable property, say, the Platonic form of Humanity? Or is it something concrete, particular, and individual, say, a flesh-and-blood composite? If the latter, what are its component parts? Does it have both a body and a soul? Just one of those two? And if it has a soul, is the Word playing the role of that soul, such that there isn't a new, distinct, created soul at the first moment of the Incarnation? If the human nature was a concrete, created body and soul composite, how could one support the orthodox claim that it wasn't a person? Did Christ assume a *fallen* human nature?

Scholars disagree concerning the answers to each of these questions. This section presents the contours of the debate, different packages of answers to the questions, and reasons for thinking that some of these answers are incompatible with Conciliar Christology.

4.1 The Human Nature Itself

Traditional Christian teaching contends that Christ assumed (a) human nature. But what's (a) human nature?[25] The two main views, which are the focus of this section, are that it is either an abstract, shareable thing or a concrete, individual substance of the same type as your or my nature. There are, of course, other notions of what the nature is. Michael Rea (2011, 149) presents a theory on which the human nature is a power. That power is shared by all humans and is a feature of humans, so in that sense, the view Rea considers is similar to the abstract view. On the other hand, that power is causally efficacious and located in space and time, and so is similar to the concrete view in those respects.

In what follows, I focus on the two main views of the human nature of Christ: the abstract view and the concrete view.[26]

---

[25] For an excellent, prolonged discussion of this question in the medieval context, see Adams (1999).

[26] For discussions of these two views of nature, see Crisp (2007b, 41), Dalmau (2016, IIA:68), Dubray (1911), and Plantinga (1999, 184). For a discussion of the historical reception of the term

4.1.1 The Abstract View

On the abstract view of human nature, the human nature is a property (or a collection of properties) the instantiation of which is both necessary and sufficient for being a human. Insofar as you and I both instantiate (have, possess) that shareable feature, you and I are both human.

On the abstract view, in becoming incarnate, the Son entered into an instantiation relationship with Humanity, and so fulfilled the necessary and sufficient conditions for being a human. He was, then, a true human, in the same sense that I'm a true human.

4.1.2 The Concrete View

On the concrete view of human nature, a human nature is a concrete, particular thing. It is, as the ecumenical councils sometimes refer to it, "flesh enlivened by a rational soul," a "holy body rationally ensouled," and "human flesh which is possessed by a rational and intellectual soul" (Tanner 1990, 41, 44, 115). On this view, the nature is not a shareable thing. It is composed of particular flesh and bones. You and I don't have the very same nature in this sense of the term. Instead, a nature is "a principle of operation … active through its powers – it causes things to happen in the real world" (Baker 2013, 37). This is a typical perennial understanding of the term "nature"; the nature is the origin (*natus*) of the activity of a thing. "Nature," in this sense, refers to the same thing as "substance" and "essence" (another word with a perennial set of meanings more broad than the contemporary analytic understanding), but picks it out as the origin of action, and not as a subsisting thing (as "substance" does) or by its definition (as "essence" does; cf. St. Thomas Aquinas, *De ente et essentia*, para. 10).

On the concrete view, in becoming incarnate, the Son united a concrete nature to his divine nature (in a relation known as the hypostatic union). Having a real, flesh-and-blood concrete nature, he was, then, a true human, in the same sense that I'm a true human.

4.1.3 A Comparison of the Abstract and Concrete Views

Readers will note that the abstract and concrete views of human nature are as far apart, ontologically speaking, as two views can be. An abstract nature like Humanity is typically viewed as shareable by many individuals, not located in space or time, unable to enter into causal relations, and possessed by substances

---

"nature," and a listing of which thinkers thought what about natures, see Pawl (2016d, chap. 2 section II.b; 2019b, chap. 1 IV.b).

as a feature. A concrete nature like Christ's "holy body rationally ensouled" is on the contrary not shareable in the way a universal like Humanity is, located in space and time, able to enter into causal relations, and not possessed as a feature – on the concrete nature view, the human nature is not related to the Word as a property to a substance.

Even if they are ontologically miles apart, we still find each view assumed or defended by major thinkers in the Christian tradition. Nevertheless, as I have argued elsewhere, the texts of Conciliar Christology offer strong reason to affirm the concrete account, for at least two reasons, which I have elsewhere dubbed the *Cyrillic* and *Leonine* arguments, based on where one finds the evidence for the arguments most explicitly asserted.[27]

The Cyrillic argument begins with the ways the nature is referred to in the councils. As noted in Section 4.1.2, the nature is referred to as a "holy body rationally ensouled." No abstract object, though, is such a thing, so the nature is best understood as a concrete object.

The Leonine argument begins with the predicates the conciliar texts say of Christ's human nature. The councils say of the human nature of Christ that it can hang on a cross, be pierced, weep, feel pity, and say, "the Father is greater than I" (Tanner 1990, 80–81). No abstract nature could do or undergo any of those activities, so the nature is best understood as a concrete object.

Even if the two views of human nature are radically different, there's a sense in which there is little disagreement between the entailments of the two views. To see this, one can coin a neutral term, say, "human element," meaning the ontological component parts of a human. For some thinkers, this human element will be wholly material.[28] For hylomorphic thinkers, it will contain both body and soul. In any case, no matter the underlying ontology of the human person, the traditional Christian will affirm that Christ had a human element. For the abstract nature theorist, having such an element will be a necessary condition for instantiating Humanity. For the concrete theorist, that human element will be nothing else than the human nature of Christ. In a similar way, Brian Leftow (2004, 279) has argued that the Word becomes incarnate in a concrete human nature if and only if the Word begins exemplifying the abstract human nature.[29] That claim is not required for the point here; rather, all that is needed is the recognition that both views require Christ to take up a human element.

---

[27] See Pawl (2016d, chap. 2 section II.b; 2019b, chap. 1 IV.b). In the following arguments I make an assumption that either the concrete view or the abstract view is correct. These two views are surely the two dominant views in the literature.

[28] Both those who think the human element is wholly immaterial and those who think it is wholly material will need to explain conciliar passages that refer to it as having both a body and soul.

[29] See also Hasker (2016, 434–435), Leftow (2004, 278), and Marmodoro and Hill (2008, 101).

Both abstract theorists and concrete theorists posit a human element for Christ. Another – traditional – name for that human element is "human nature." So, for the remainder of this Element, I use the term "human nature" to refer to the human element of Christ. If the need arises to refer to the abstract nature, in order to avoid equivocation, I refer to it as "Humanity."

4.2 The Parts of Christ's Human Nature

Christ's human element, the concrete human nature of Christ, is typically thought to have parts. As quoted in Section 4.1.2, Conciliar Christology lists some of those parts as a body and a rational and intellectual soul. It included hands and feet that were pierced, blood, and all the other component parts of a typical human being. At least that's the orthodox view. There are other views, though, concerning Christ's human nature.

4.2.1 The Body of Christ

The view that Christ lacked a body is traditionally referred to as "Docetism" (from the Greek word meaning "to appear"). On this view, Christ merely appeared to have a human body or to be a human. Such a view makes little sense of the scriptural passages concerning Christ's physical activities. Moreover, Christ sometimes seems to act in ways intended to show that he really does have a body, as when he asks for some fish to eat after the resurrection (Luke 24:41–43), or when he allows Thomas to put his hand into his side (John 20:27).

Another extreme view with respect to Christ's body argues that the person of the Word *transformed* from being immaterial to being a human material body, or a human animal. Kevin Sharpe (2017, 118) writes that "the Son's becoming human was a matter of his being transformed into a human and not merely his assumption of a concrete human nature."[30] Such a transformational view has a dubious pedigree in Christology. As Cyril says in his second letter to Nestorius, accepted at the Council of Ephesus,

> For we do not say that the nature of the Word was changed and became flesh, *nor that he was turned into a whole man made of body and soul.* Rather do we claim that the Word in an unspeakable, inconceivable manner united to himself hypostatically flesh enlivened by a rational soul, and so became man and was called son of man. (Tanner 1990, 41, emphasis added)

---

[30] For discussion of this or similar views, see Arcadi (2018, 4), Crisp (2009, chap. 7), Jaeger (2017), Leftow (2015), Lim (2019), Merricks (2007), Turner (2017) and van Horn (2010).

Similarly, Leo says in his *Tome*, "the Word is not the same thing as the flesh" (Tanner 1990, 81). Both views, then – that Christ lacked a body and that he was *transformed* into a human being – are precluded by Conciliar Christology.

4.2.2 The Soul of Christ

The view that Christ lacked a created, human soul is traditionally referred to as "Apollinarianism," after its most famous advocate, Apollinaris (the younger) of Laodicea. Some thinkers, seeing that if Christ had a created, human soul, then he'd have two centers of cognition (one divine, one human), worried that there would be two distinct persons there, contrary to biblical witness and traditional teaching. In order to safeguard Christ's having a soul, but also to remove the alleged problems of his having two faculties by which to reason or will, these thinkers had the person of the Word himself play the role of Christ's soul. So, on such a view, Christ has a soul (the Word), yet only one set of intellective powers.

One finds such a view in Moreland and Craig (2003, 611), where they note that the councils preclude it, but claim that the Scriptures allow it.[31] Craig has called this view "Neo-Apollinarianism," and said that it includes the claim that

> The soul of the human nature of Christ is the second person of the Trinity, the Logos. The human nature of Christ is composed of the Logos and a human body. (Harris and Craig n.d.)

What ought one to make of these views, where the divine person is the human soul of Christ?

The main objections to such a view are the following. First, the soul is that which makes a human *to be* human. Lacking a human soul, then, Christ wouldn't be truly human. Second, consider the maxim of St. Gregory of Nazianzus that what is not assumed is not healed. Were there no assumed human soul, then, there would be no healing of our human souls by the Incarnation. For these and other similar reasons, Apollinarianism was declared a heresy at the second ecumenical council, the First Council of Constantinople in AD 381, and reaffirmed as a heresy many times over in later councils.

Concerning whether Neo-Apollinarianism is distinct from Apollinarianism in anything more than name, note how a church council in Rome in AD 382 condemned Apollinaris's view:

> We pronounce anathema against them who say that the Word of God is in the human flesh in lieu and place of the human rational and intellective soul. For, the Word of God is the Son Himself. Neither did He come in the flesh to

---

[31] Rea (2011, 149–150) presents without endorsement such a view.

replace, but rather to assume and preserve from sin and save the rational and intellective soul of man. (as quoted in Sollier 1907)

Neo-Apollinarianism is the doctrine that, eight years before his death, Apollinaris was condemned for teaching.

Recall the quotation at the end of Section 4.2.1. It claims that the thing united to the Son in the Incarnation was "flesh enlivened by a rational soul." If the soul were the Logos, the person of the Son, then the Son unites to himself flesh enlivened by himself. Such a doubled union – Son to flesh, then Son to (Son and flesh) – is unheard of in Christological discussions.[32]

Finally, recall the worry that partially motivates acceptance of Apollinarianism – if there were two centers of intellection, then there'd be two persons there.[33] Such a worry rightly attempts to safeguard the unity of the person of Christ, which is a necessary condition of traditional Christology. At the same time, though, another necessary condition of traditional Christology is dyothelitism, the claim that Christ had two distinct wills, a human will and a divine will. For instance, the sixth ecumenical council, the Third Council of Constantinople, includes an exposition of faith that affirms:

> [T]he difference of the natures [is] made known in the same one subsistence
> in that each nature wills and performs the things that are proper to it in
> a communication with the other; then in accord with this reasoning we hold
> that two natural wills and principles of action meet in correspondence for the
> salvation of the human race. (Tanner 1990, 129–130)

Here the traditional texts teach that there are two natures, and they are known because each has its own, distinct will. As such, even if one worries that two wills implies two persons, the response of denying two wills is not an open option for the proponent of Conciliar Christology.

Some have attempted to read this passage as consistent with Christ having a single will that counts as both divine and human. In this attenuated sense, though numerically one, Christ has two wills. Such a reading would allow the proponent of traditional Christology to avoid the two-person worry and yet maintain consistency with the councils. Crisp (2007b, 59–60) and I (Pawl 2016d, 19–20) argue that this reading is inconsistent with other claims the councils make concerning Christ's wills. The divine will leads the human will, which is subjugated to it; each nature has a will and operates through it, etc. Such claims are difficult to parse if there is only one will.

---

[32] For more on the topic of a double union, see Pawl (2016d, 48–50).

[33] For more on the topic of whether two minds or wills implies two persons, see Pawl (2016d, chap. 9).

Given that Conciliar Christology does teach the unity of the person, along with the duality of natures, each with its own will and operation, how does the Christian avoid the objection that there are, in fact, two persons in Christ?

4.3 Was Christ's Human Nature a Person in Its Own Right?

The answer to the question in this subheading is "no" for all traditional Christian thinkers, as the opposing view, which often goes under the name "Nestorianism," was condemned at the Council of Ephesus in AD 431. The human nature is not a hypostasis at all, and so not a person, since all persons are hypostases. That said, the question still arose concerning the relation the human nature bore to personhood. Was the human nature entirely non-hypostatic (*anhypostatic*), or was it instead hypostasized *in* and *by* the person of the Word (*enhypostatic*)? The orthodox answer was that the nature is personal (*enhypostatic*), but it is itself neither a person (*hypostatic*) nor wholly impersonal (*anhypostatic*).[34] The reason given for these views, though, is different for different schools of thought.

For those who believe the human nature to be an abstract entity, Humanity, the answer is easy: no abstract, shareable thing is a person in its own right. In fact, on the abstract view, it is hard to see how this perennial Christological worry concerning the human nature of Christ could be taken seriously. But even still, people who affirm an abstract nature believe that Jesus has a full component of human parts, such as his body, hair, skin, blood, etc. Take all those human parts together, which I referred to in Section 4.1.3 as Christ's human element: why isn't that thing a person?

If, contrary to orthodox Christianity, one denies that Christ had a created human soul, then there is again an easy answer. The full human element of Jesus was without any second thing that operated rationally. Thus, there's little motivation to worry that the nature might fulfill the conditions for itself being a person. The word "full" in "full human element" becomes questionable at this point, though.

Consider, then, those who think that the full human element, the concrete human nature of Christ, had all the same types of ontological components that yours or mine does. Suppose, as the councils say, it had its own intellectual faculties, its own will and operation, as we saw in Section 4.2.2. In such a case, why isn't it a person?

By the medieval era, two main schools had emerged in answer to this question.[35] More than 100 years ago, Charles Dubray (1911) put the division well:

---

[34] For more on the *enhypostatic/anhypostatic* distinction, see Crisp (2007b, chap. 3).

[35] For more on these two schools, see Hipp (2001, 471–518) and Pawl (2016d, 68–70).

> The Human Nature in Christ is complete and perfect as nature, yet it lacks that which would make it a person, whether this be something negative, as Scotists hold, namely the mere fact that a nature is not assumed by a higher person, or, as Thomists assert, some positive reality distinct from nature and making it incommunicable.

The next two subsections discuss these views.

4.3.1 The Thomistic View

One view, often associated with St. Thomas Aquinas, is that being a person requires a certain component part. Christ's human nature, on this view, lacks that ontological component, and so fails to be a person.[36]

What exactly the part is differs in different views. Some call it a mode, others an individual act of existence, others still something else. For the purposes of responding to the charge that the human nature of Christ is a person in its own right, the ontological category that the thing falls under is not as important as the method of response. Christ's human nature lacks an ontological component that it would need to have in order to be a person, and so it fails to be a person.

4.3.2 The Scotistic View

The Scotistic view posits a negative condition for personhood. For a nature to be a person, it has to be unassumed. Since Christ's human nature fails that condition, since it is assumed, it does not count as a person. This view does not require the supposition that your or my nature has a certain ontological doodad in virtue of which we are persons. Instead, it merely requires our natures to be unassumed for us to count as persons.

4.3.3 A Similarity between the Views

One might pause here to reflect on a similarity between these views. Given orthodox Christology, as we see in the next section, there is something referred to as a hypostatic union. St. Thomas Aquinas and many others view that union as itself a created thing, something had, in some sense, by Christ's human nature. If that's the case – if Christ's human nature has a special ontological component in virtue of which it is assumed, then we get similarity between the Thomistic and Scotistic views. Letting "CHN" abbreviate "Christ's human nature," consider the claim "CHN is a person" and its negation, "it is false that CHN is a person." The Thomist requires CHN to have an additional

---

[36] Textual evidence indicatess, though, that Aquinas held a view much closer to the Scotistic view discussed later in this Element. See Pawl and Spencer (2016, 148–149).

ontological component for the first claim to be true. In the language of truth makers, it is CHN *plus the component* that makes "CHN is a person" true. Such a component is a necessary condition, and so in worlds where CHN lacks a component, for instance, the actual world, "CHN is a person" is false. The Scotist requires CHN to have an additional ontological component for the second claim to be true. In the language of truth makers, it is CHN *plus the hypostatic union* that makes "it is false that CHN is a person" true. Such a hypostatic union is a necessary condition for the truth of that claim, and so in worlds where CHN exists but lacks a hypostatic union, "it is false that CHN is a person" is false – in other words, in such worlds, "CHN is a person" is true. Both theories, then, require some ontological doodad in virtue of which one or other of the contradictory predications about personhood is true.

4.4 Was Christ's Human Nature Fallen or Unfallen?

This question is vexed.[37] It is vexed in part because the word "fallen" is understood in different ways in different traditions. Fallen from what, to what, in what respect? In a diminished sense of the term, every traditional Christian agrees that Christ's human nature was weakened, insofar as, while it was still of the very same type as Adam and Eve's human natures, it lacked certain good-making features of those natures in their original state. Many Christian thinkers have claimed that Adam and Eve had certain *preternatural gifts* in the garden, such as full control over their bodily passions and immortality (see Aquinas's *Summa theologiae* I, qq. 94–97 for more on these gifts). Jesus did not have all of these gifts – for instance, he wasn't immortal according to his humanity – and so, in that respect, his human nature was weakened.

On the other hand, for some thinkers, to say that Christ's human nature was fallen is to say that, in virtue of it, Christ was potentially sinful. Oliver Crisp (2007b, chap. 4; 2004) understands fallenness in this more robust way when he claims that Christ's having a fallen human nature would be catastrophic for traditional Christian thinking, as fallenness implies having Original Sin – a hereditary corruption or stain that results from the first sin of our ancestors (see Crisp 2007b, 107).

The traditional answer to the question of whether Christ had a fallen nature can be put in a way that garners broad consensus. Christ had a human nature that was corruptible. That said, he did not have Original Sin, neither did he have the actual ability to sin (for more on the ability to sin, see Section 6.1.2). There is disagreement on whether such a state can rightly be called "fallen." Some think

---

[37] For more recent work on this question, see (2019), McFarland (2008), King (2015), McCall (2019, chap. 4), and McFarland(2008)

fallenness requires Original Sin, others that it merely requires not having all the preternatural gifts that Adam had. How much of a fall is required to count as a fallen human nature is a question we need not answer at this point.

We find others drawing these distinctions in the understanding of fallenness as well. Immediately before offering pages of quotations verifying the claim, Alfeyev writes:

> Many pronouncements of the Eastern fathers, including Irenaeus of Lyons, Athanasius of Alexandria, Gregory of Nyssa, Cyril of Alexandria, and Gregory Palamas, leave no doubt that these fathers considered Christ's human nature, with the exception of sin, to be like the nature of fallen man. It is from the fallen, and not the first-formed Adam, that Christ inherited a corrupted, mortal, impassioned nature. (Alfeyev 2012, 278)

He goes on in the same section to claim that, for the Orthodox, Christ did not have personal sin, sinful inclination, or Original Sin.[38]

4.5 The Weaknesses and Infirmities of Christ's Human Nature

On the traditional view, Christ had weaknesses and infirmities during life. As Scripture notes, he was at times hungry, sad, anxious, thirsty, etc. St. John of Damascus claims that such "innocent" passions were not lacking in him. Just as traditional is the affirmation that Christ lacked sinfully disordered passions. For instance, consider a sinful inclination to some deplorable type of action (the reader can supply her own). Such deplorable inclinations evince a faulty moral character, though not one that is necessarily blameworthy, depending on the source of the inclination. Such dispositions were lacking in Christ, it is argued, because to have them is to have a moral fault, and no one who is God could have a moral fault. The relation between sinfulness, passions, and temptation is the topic of Section 6.1.2.

4.6 Conclusion

This section explored various divisions in the conceptualization of Christ's human nature. One might think of it as abstract or concrete. If concrete, then there are further choices to be made about the number of parts it has, and the person's relation to that nature. If the nature is concrete, with both a rational soul and a body (as Conciliar Christology teaches), then the question of whether it is a person must be addressed. Two reasons for denying the nature's personhood that this section canvasses are that it lacks some component part necessary for

---

[38] Alfeyev (2012, 285) notes that the notion of "Original Sin" in Western contexts isn't the same as in Eastern contexts, and in neither sense did Christ have Original Sin.

personhood (the so-called Thomistic view) or that it satisfies some condition, assumption, incompatible with personhood (the so-called Scotistic view). Concerning fallenness, one must specify what exactly is meant by that term. If fallenness merely means that it doesn't have some good-making qualities that Adam's pre-fallen nature had, then Christ's human nature is fallen, since it was mortal. If fallenness goes further and requires Original Sin, concupiscence, and liability to actually sinning, then traditionally the human nature assumed by Christ is not fallen in that particular sense of the term.

5 The Hypostatic Union

This section focuses on the union that holds between the two natures in the one person of the Word. What can we say of the union? What features does it have? What role does it play in the Incarnation?[39]

5.1 The Features of the Hypostatic Union

The conciliar documents contain more about what the union isn't than about what it is. It was not merely by "God's will alone or good pleasure," nor by "a conjunction of dignity or authority or power," nor by a mixing of natures, nor by affection, nor a union of adoration or honor, nor a union as one finds "between a man and his wife" (Tanner 1990, 41, 59, 115–116, 119). In uniting, the two natures undergo "no confusion, no change, no division, no separation" (Tanner 1990, 86). Moreover, the union is, according to the councils, ineffable (Tanner 1990, 72, 117). It was brought about in "an unspeakable, inconceivable manner" (Tanner 1990, 41). These claims about ineffability and inconceivability are not meant by the conciliar fathers in such a robust sense that we cannot say or think anything at all about the union. After all, they do say many things about it, as we see in the next paragraph. Rather, they mean that it is *impossible* for us to completely grasp or understand the union.[40]

So much by way of negation. What can be said of the union positively? The hypostatic union is the union that holds, in the person of the Word, between the divine and human natures, in virtue of which Christ is one person of two natures. The relata of the hypostatic union are, on the divine side, the divine nature, and, on the human side, the human nature, or its parts.[41] Elsewhere, the councils refer to the hypostatic union as a union of "subsistence" or "synthesis" (Tanner 1990,

---

[39] For a more detailed discussion of the hypostatic union in the conciliar texts, see Pawl (2016d, 20–23).

[40] For more on the meaning of ineffability, see Pawl (2020, sec. 2). For more on mystery and philosophical reflection on the incarnation, see Pawl (2016d, 88–91; 2019b, 5–6).

[41] For more on whether the human relatum is properly characterized as the full human nature or the parts of the human nature, see Pawl (2019b, 109–113).

115). The two natures are united, in the traditional language, in the person of the Word, but the person of the Word is not, technically speaking, one of the relata of the relationship. (The term used for the relation of the Word to the human nature is *assumption*.) It is important that the union does not take a *person* on the human side of the relation, as discussed in Section 4.3. Were it to do so, there would be two different persons in the Incarnation, rather than one person who is both God and human, as the Nicene Creed claims.

It is this fact – the fact that there is one person who is both divine and human, having both divine and human natures – that grounds the Communication of Idioms.

5.2 The Communication of Idioms

The Communication of Idioms (*Communicatio Idiomatum*) is a thesis about language. It is the thesis that what we can say truthfully of the one person of Christ in virtue of one nature, we can say when referring to Christ with a subject term drawn from the other nature.[42] For instance, it is true that Christ was born of Mary. And that predicate, "born of Mary," is true of him, not in virtue of something that happened to the divine nature, but rather in virtue of something that happened to his human nature, that flesh-and-blood reality. Christ, though, is God, and is God in virtue of his divine nature, not his human nature. Nevertheless, we can put together a true claim using terms apt of him due to different natures, as when we say that God was born of Mary.[43] This, of course, is the very case that got Nestorius in trouble, since he wanted to affirm that while Mary bore Christ, she did not bear God. Such a claim – that Mary bore Christ, but she did not bear God – Cyril and others reasonably argued, would imply that the person, Christ, is not a divine person. Additional examples of the Communication of Idioms, both found in Aquinas, are "A man created the stars" and "The God of glory was crucified" (*ST.* III q.16 a.4). In both cases, a predicate term apt of the one person in virtue of one nature is paired with a subject term apt of the person in virtue of the other nature to make a true claim about the one God-man, Jesus Christ.

We find support for the Communication of Idioms in the conciliar texts. We already saw one supporting text at the beginning of Section 2.1. We see another at the end of Section 7.4.2. For a third, Cyril includes in his third letter to Nestorius the following anathema:

---

[42] For more on the Communication of Idioms, see de Aldama and Solano (2014, 170–171), Cross (2019), Pawl (2016d, 23–27, 54–55, 62–65; 2019b, 17–19), and Pohle (1913, 186).

[43] I am using the term "apt" to mean *correctly assertible of*. Some thinkers say a term is *true* of a subject. That language is acceptable, too, but I prefer to avoid it, as I take *truth* to be a feature of a complete proposition, not a feature of a term in a proposition.

> If anyone distributes between the two persons or hypostases the expressions used either in the gospels or in the apostolic writings, whether they are used by the holy writers of Christ or by him about himself, and ascribes some to him as to a man, thought of separately from the Word from God, and others, as befitting God, to him as to the Word from God the Father, let him be anathema. (Tanner 1990, 59)

Here Cyril, in a text accepted at the Council of Ephesus, asserts that the expressions ascribed to Christ as human are ascribed to the very same subject as the expressions ascribed to him as God.

It should be clear that the Communication of Idioms doctrine as spelled out here does not imply that a predicate truthfully said of one nature is thus truthfully assertible of the other nature, or that a predicate truthfully said of the person is thus truthfully assertible of either nature.[44] From Christ's being crucified, we cannot derive that his divine nature was crucified. From Christ's human nature being pierced on the wood of the cross, as Chalcedon teaches (see Section 4.1.3), we cannot derive that the divine nature was pierced.

Likewise, the Communication of Idioms does not undergird either of the following two theses:

1. Any predicate truly said of either nature of Christ is also truly said of the person of Christ.
2. Any predicate truly said of the person of Christ is truly said of at least one nature of Christ.

Neither of these is true, we can see, since they have counterexamples. Christ's human nature is truly said to be "identical to a human nature," and there is a time before which it did not exist, but neither of these predicates is truly said of the person of Christ. The person of Christ is not "*identical* to the human nature," and, though there was a time before he was human, there was no time before which that person did not exist (the original Nicene Creed precludes such a claim with its final anathema). Likewise, the second claim is subject to counterexample. One predicate truly said of the person of Christ is that he is "one person in two natures." But neither the divine nor the human nature is "one person in two natures." We find, then, that neither of these theses survives scrutiny.

In fact, the notion of "communication" may be misleading here, even if it is the traditional language. It is not that the term goes from the nature to the person, as a migratory bird might go from one location to another. Rather, it is that the incarnate person fulfills the ontological conditions that are needful in typical cases to satisfy the predicate, and that very same incarnate person can be

---

[44] Though some Lutheran theologians have taught such communication from nature to nature; see Pohle (1913, 194–195) for one discussion of this.

referred to by terms that refer to him in virtue of his other nature. So we can use a subject term from one nature, since the very person referred to by that term satisfies the truth conditions for the predicate. It should not be thought of as a predicate or a property migrating from one subject, whether linguistic or ontological, to another. Rather, it should be thought of in terms of fulfilling truth conditions or not.

5.3 Models of the Hypostatic Union

Even if the hypostatic union is ineffable, as we saw that Conciliar Christology claims in Section 5.1, one could still ask whether a viable model exists for it, or a helpful analogy.

Thomas Flint (2011, 71–79) draws a division between models of the incarnation that has become standard.[45] On Model T:

> In becoming human, the Son or Word of God (whom I'll label W) takes on CHN as a part. This assumption results in a Son who combines both his original divine substance (D) and his created human nature (CHN). (Flint 2011, 71)

On Model T, the Word comes to have an additional part (or part-like thing): the human nature.

On the second model, Model A:

> The Son unites himself to CHN in the Incarnation. But the composite thus formed is not the Son. The Son remains simply one part of the composite entity that results from his assuming a human nature. That composite entity, which (following Scotus and Leftow) we can call Christ, is a contingent thing, composed of another contingent entity (CHN) and of a necessary one (the Son). (Flint 2011, 79)

On Model A, a contingent entity called "Christ" comes into existence, which is itself composed of two things – the preexistent Word and the created human nature. Is there reason to favor one view over the other?

There are good reasons to prefer Model T to Model A. First is a reason based on the proper relata for the hypostatic union. What two things are united in the union? The councils say that "a union of two natures took place," and "one and the same Christ, Son, Lord, only-begotten [is] acknowledged in two natures," and "two different natures come together to form a unity, and from both arose one Christ, one Son" (Tanner 1990, 70, 86, 41, respectively). Model A has the

---

[45] For discussion of these two compositional models of the Incarnation, see Crisp (2011; 2016, chap. 6), Flint (2015), Hasker (2015), Leftow (2011, 321), and Turner (2019 n 5).

person of the Son, not the divine nature, as one of the relata, while Model T has the natures as the two relata. Score one for Model T.

Second is a reason from the nature of personhood. On Model A, a whole (the contingent composite, Christ) has a person (the Word) as a part. But on the traditional view of personhood, explicated in Section 2.1, a person cannot be a part of a larger whole. Thus, Model A sits uneasily with the traditional notion of personhood.[46]

We might also ask about helpful analogies in addition to models. The Athanasian Creed (Denzinger 2002, para. 40) and the Council of Ephesus (Tanner 1990, 52) both use the analogy that as a man's soul indwells his body, so likewise the Word indwells the human nature. Katherin Rogers (2010; 2013) offers an analogy based on virtual realities. A child can play a video game and in doing so enter and act in a virtual world through the character in the game; similarly, the Son, through taking up a created human nature, can enter and act in the created world.[47]

5.4 Conclusion

This section presented an account of what the hypostatic union is not, then some discussion of what the union does. The main theological work the union does is ontologically undergirding the union between the two natures in one person, and so providing an explanation for the Communication of Idioms. The union has been modeled in myriad ways, including models based on a mereological understanding of the union, a union of body and soul, and multiple sci-fi analogies.

Having discussed the ontology of the person, the natures, and their union, now we move on to discuss the activities of that person.

6 The Activities of Christ

This section focuses on the activity of Christ. What philosophical questions arise from this activity? The main contemporary discussions of Christ's activities might be grouped under three headings: with respect to his acts of will, his acts of intellect, and his death.

6.1 Volitional Activities

According to traditional teaching, as noted earlier (Section 4.2.2), Christ has two wills, one divine and one human. This duality of wills gives rise to

---

[46] For a reply to these objections to Model A, see Crisp (2011, 52–56).

[47] Hasker (2017) gives a similar example in terms of the sci-fi movie *Avatar*.

questions about what each will can do and their interrelations. Was each will free? Or, perhaps put differently: was the one Christ free with respect to each will? Moreover, given that Christ had a human will, could he sin by means of that human will? If not, as was traditionally believed, what implications does that inability to sin have on his being tempted? In this section, I consider each of these questions.

6.1.1 Was Christ Free?

The consensus in Christian thinking has been that Christ has two volitional powers, a divine one and a human one, and that he can will freely with each will.[48] Such an answer has led to two types of objections: objections from the interrelation of the wills and objections from volitional activities and personhood.

Considering objections from the interrelation of the wills, one might well wonder here what the relations are between the two wills of Christ. The texts of Conciliar Christology are not silent on this issue. For instance, the Third Council of Constantinople (681) says:

> We proclaim equally two natural volitions or wills in him and two natural principles of action which undergo no division, no change, no partition, no confusion, in accordance with the teaching of the holy fathers. And the two natural wills not in opposition, as the impious heretics said, far from it, but his human will following, and not resisting or struggling, rather in fact subject to his divine and all powerful will. (Tanner 1990, 128)

Here the human will is said to follow, be subject to, not resist, and not struggle against, the divine will. As Richard Swinburne (1994, 198–199) and Garrett Deweese (2007, 133), among others, wonder: how can a will be free in such a state?[49]

The main question at this point is how strong the subjugation is. My children might follow my will in a certain thing, say, cleaning their rooms, without resisting or struggling. (I imagine that this is possible.) In doing so, they don't render themselves unfree. What is needed for the objection to succeed is some reason to think that Christ's human will is subjugated

---

[48] See Pawl (2019b, 119–123), Pawl and Timpe (2016), and Wessling (2013) for more discussion of this issue.

[49] See Pawl (2019b, 126–131) for a detailed discussion of this objection and a reply. For a critical discussion of Swinburne and Deweese, see Pawl (2016d, 219–220). For other discussions of Christ's freedom, see Gaine (2015b, chap. 7), Hebblethwaite (2008, 68), Hick (2006, 56), Kereszty (2002, 392–396), McFarland (2007), McKinley (2015), Rogers (2016), and Sturch (1991, 29, 167).

in a much stronger way, as, perhaps, a hypnotized person's will is subjugated to the hypnotizer.[50]

It is true that the examples just offered – a parent and child, a hypnotizer and the one hypnotized – are examples of two different persons and their own wills, and not examples of one person with two distinct wills. This is understandable, as no other example of a two-willed person exists that we can employ. If there is some reason to think that having two wills in a single person adds difficulties with respect to this objection from subjugation, above and beyond those found in the two-person examples employed, the reason is still to be given.

What of the second variety of worries, the personhood worries? If there are two distinct wills, how are there not two distinct persons? The reader does well to remember the traditional definition of "person" employed in these debates. A person, as expressed in Section 2.1, is a supposit with a rational nature. Since, as argued in Section 4.3, the human nature does not fulfill the condition for being a supposit, that nature does not satisfy the conditions for being a person. So there are not two persons in the relevant sense of "person."[51]

6.1.2 Could Christ Sin?

The consensus answer to the question of whether Christ could sin with either of his wills is "no." One might wonder how the inability to sin is consistent with the freedom of both of Christ's wills. Moreover, one might also wonder how he could be tempted, if willing something sinful was impossible for him.

Concerning whether Christ could sin, contemporary literature has featured extended discussion. The traditional teaching is that Christ is not only sinless but also impeccable.[52] If he is impeccable, does that render him not omnipotent, owing to the fact that there is something – that is, sinning – which Christ cannot do?[53] Typically, the answer is "no": being able to sin is not its own power,

---

[50] For an argument for strong subjugation from a different starting point, see Werther (2005).

[51] A reader might accuse this response of defining away the problem, rather than facing it head on. Such a reader does well to remember that the concept of "person" I employ here is the traditional understanding of it in these contexts. If the objector understands personhood differently, and so sees this as a devastating objection, it is the objector who is defining terms advantageously. I consider this worry at length in chapter 9 of Pawl (2016). See also Murray and Rea (2008, 82–84).

[52] On the historical affirmation of impeccability, see Bavinck (2006, 314), O'Collins (1995, 281), Pohle (1913, 214), Schmaus (1971, 259), and Weis (2003).

[53] On the question of whether God can sin, see, for instance, Adams (2006, 75–79), Brümmer (1984), Carter (1985), Funkhouser (2006), Garcia (1987), Gellman (1977), Leftow (1989), Morris (1983) and Stump (2005, 102–7)

a power had by you but lacked by God.[54] To sin is to use a power poorly, but sinning is not its own power, and so, the typical answer goes, God's inability to sin is not the lack of some power had by others. As T. J. Mawson (2018, 42) puts the point, the ability to sin is a liability, not a power, and so not a lack of power if it is missing. God, as a perfect being, has all powers and no liabilities.

Concerning whether Christ could be tempted, again, the discussion is vast.[55] The traditional view is that Christ could be tempted, as Scripture (e.g., Hebrews 4:15) and the councils say, yet Christ could not sin. How can one make sense of such a conjunction of claims?

One might attempt to explain the temptation of an impeccable person in various ways. First, one might distinguish between internal and external temptation. Christ could be externally tempted – the devil might wave a good in front of his nose – yet neither feel the internal, sinful impulses toward that temptation nor be able to succumb to them.[56] In such a case, it would be true to say he is tempted (in the external sense) and such a temptation would not require his ability to sin.

A second response is known as the epistemic response. To be tempted, on this view, does not require the actual ability to sin; it merely requires that *one believe that one has* the actual ability to sin.[57] You might be duped into thinking that you have the launch button for the Russian nuclear program. And you might feel sorely tempted to make use of that button, even though you don't, in fact, have the ability to launch the missiles. This response requires that Christ not know of his divine status and mission, such that he mistakenly thinks that he is a person able to sin. Such a view is precluded by traditional views of Christ's knowledge, as we see in Section 6.2.1. Nevertheless, this remains an open option for those not wed to the traditional views of Christ's knowledge.

A third response is to conceptualize temptation such that it doesn't require either the ability to sin or even the belief that one can sin. Rather, following

---

[54] For more on this point, see McKinley (2009, 258), Morris (1986, 167), and Pawl (2019b, 151–153) and the works in the previous footnote.

[55] On the questions of temptation and sin, see Canham (2000, 95), Couenhoven (2012, 406–407), Crisp (2007b; 2007c), Davidson (2008, 395), Erickson (1996, 562), Fisk (2007), Gaine (2015b, 168–172), Hart (1995), King (2015, 73–76), McKinley (2009; 2011), Morris (1987, chap. 7), Murray and Rea (2008, 82–90), O'Collins (1995, 283–284), Pawl (2019b, chap. 6), Pelser (2019), Sturch (1991, 19–20), Swinburne (1994, 204–207), Ware (2013, chap. 5), Wellum (2016, 459–465), and Werther (1993; 2012).

[56] Both Aquinas (2013, bks. 4, lecture 1, pg 101) and Crisp (2007c, 178) argue that Christ's temptations have an external source. See Murray and Rea (2008, 86) and Pawl (2019b, 150–151) for more discussion of this view.

[57] For discussions of this view, see Bartel (1995, 154–55), Hart (1995, 41), McKinley (2009, 239–243), Morris (1987, 147–148), O'Collins (1995, 283–284), and Pawl (2019b, 139–143).

some psychological discussion in the literature on temptation, we might think of temptation as follows:

Temptation:	An affectively charged cognitive event in which an object or activity that is associated with pleasure or relief of discomfort is in focal attention, yet the object of that desire conflicts with the person's values and goals. (Pawl 2019b, 144)[58]

Here, the affectively charged "pull" of temptation need not take something sinful as its object. It might be the pleasure of the taste of a chocolate cake that is in focal attention, yet that good is seen to conflict with a distal goal – the goal, say, of losing weight via dieting. On this view, Christ could have the pull toward food in the desert, or away from the discomfort of crucifixion, and yet judge such pleasure or lack of discomfort as contrary to his goal of fasting or his plan of atonement for sinful humanity. On this psychological view, then, neither the ability to sin nor the belief that one can sin is a necessary condition for temptation.

The tradition makes a distinction between "natural and innocent" passions and those that are not.[59] Some passions, such as fear, hunger, thirst, aversion, sadness, and so on are blameless and natural to humans. These are passions Christ might have, and they are a blameless basis for temptation, when understood as outlined in this section. Other passions, as discussed by Oliver Crisp (2007a, 176), are evil in themselves. Such vicious passions (e.g., urges to sexually assault others) show an imperfect character. The view under discussion here has it that Christ never had any such passions or appetitive pulls, and so no internal temptation toward them.

6.2 Intellectual Activities

Just as Christ's having both a divine and a human will gives rise to questions concerning the states and interactions of those wills, so likewise his having both a divine and a human intellect raises similar questions. Christ had two faculties of knowing: a divine one and a human one. What did Christ know with respect to those intellects? When did he know it? Did such knowledge raise new problems for his freedom?

---

[58] See Hoffman et al. (2012, 1319), Kavanaugh, Andrade, and May (2005, 447), and Milyavskaya et al (2015, 678) for relevant psychological discussion. See Pawl (2019b, 143–51) for a detailed explication of the psychological view of temptation. Something similar to this view of temptation is at work in Aquinas's thought as well; see Gondreau (2018, 359).

[59] See Alfeyev (2012, 283) and John of Damascus (1958, 323–324).

6.2.1 What Did Christ Know, and When?

Since Christ, on the traditional Christian picture, had two intellects, one divine and one human, the discussion of his knowledge is typically divided into the knowledge that he had in virtue of his divine intellect, and the knowledge that he had in virtue of his assumed human intellect.[60] Concerning the divine intellect, the traditional view is that Christ was omniscient. Anything there is to be known, Christ knew it via his divine intellect, just as the Father and Holy Spirit do.

Concerning his human intellect, the traditional view is that Christ had three types of human knowledge, in addition to his divine knowledge. He had the beatific vision, as the blessed in heaven do, he had infused knowledge, and he had acquired knowledge. Beatific knowledge is knowledge had by union, participation, or similarity with God.[61] It is qualitatively distinct from our mundane forms of knowing. Infused and acquired knowledge are alike in all ways except cause. The difference is that infused knowledge is imparted directly by a divine act, whereas acquired knowledge is acquired as human knowledge is typically acquired. If you learn my paternal grandmother's first name via my telling you, that's acquired knowledge.[62] If you learn it by God "zapping it in," that's infused knowledge.

Aquinas, for just one example, posits this fourfold distinction in types of knowledge of Christ (see *ST* III. q. 9). Why include all four types? The divine type is easy to explain for non-kenotic thinkers. Christ retained his divine dignities when incarnate. One divine dignity is omniscience. So he remained omniscient as he eternally was – in virtue of his divine intellect. Concerning the beatific knowledge, the question of whether Christ had it is more vexed, even among traditional Catholic thinkers.[63] Typical arguments in its favor often go as follows. Christ is the author of salvation for humans, which consists in the beatific vision. But Christ cannot give a perfection that Christ does not have. So he must have it. Another argument comes from fittingness: it is unfitting for the source of the beatific vision to lack it.[64] Concerning infused knowledge, Aquinas argues from Scripture, for instance, Colossians 2:3, which says that in Christ "are hid all the treasures of wisdom and knowledge."[65] Finally, what of acquired knowledge?

---

[60] For discussions of Christ's knowledge, see Denzinger (2002, 2184–2185, 2289), Gaine (2015a, 2015b, chap. 6;), Green (2017), Loke (2013), Margerie (1980), Moloney (2000), Rosenberg (2010), Scarpelli (2007), and Wellum (2016, 454–459).

[61] For more on the mode of beatific knowledge, see Aquinas's Compendium of Theology, 216, ST III q.9 a.3 ad.3, and *ST* III q.10 a.4 resp.

[62] Marge.

[63] For discussion of this controversy, see Weinandy (2004; 2014) and White (2005; 2016, chap. 5).

[64] These are both sketches of arguments that Aquinas gives. See *ST* III. q.9 a.2 *resp.*; *Comp. Theol.* 216.

[65] See *ST* III. q.9 a.3 *sed contra*.

Recall that, on the traditional doctrine, Christ has a created human soul, the same in type as yours or mine. Now, your soul and mine has natural activities, some of which are intellectual. Were Christ to lack all acquired knowledge, a standard activity and perfection of a human soul would be lacking in him. It would be there, but "offline," so to speak. This appears unfitting to many thinkers. So, like typical humans, Christ could use his intellect to know things.

How can we explain the biblical passages that seem to require ignorance of Christ, then? Consider, for instance, these two passages:[66]

> Luke 2:52: And Jesus increased in wisdom and in stature, and in favor with God and man.

> Mark 13:32: [Jesus said,] "But of that day or that hour no one knows, not even the angels in heaven, nor the Son, but only the Father."

Historically, there are three main ways to deal with such passages.

First, a recent way of responding has been to suppose that Christ was really ignorant of things like when he would return. Kenotic thinkers can claim that Christ in no way knew when he would return, owing to the fact that he emptied himself of his divine knowledge.

Second, some can claim that when Christ claimed lack of knowledge, he meant that he lacked knowledge *in his human intellect*, not that he lacked knowledge *full stop*.

Third, and more traditional, is the attempt to deny that such passages really require ignorance. We find this variety of response in Cyril of Alexandria, Gregory the Great, John Chrysostom, Augustine, Maximus the Confessor, and Thomas Aquinas, to name just some thinkers who support this method of response.[67] Concerning the passage from Luke, Christ grew in *appearance of* or *renown for* wisdom and favor with God, and also in *acquired knowledge*. This growth in acquired knowledge is not a change from ignorance to knowledge; rather, it is coming *in a new way* to know something already known. Concerning the passage from Mark, these authors distinguish between the state of knowing and the revelatory act of making known. Christ here, they claim, intends to say that he does not *make known* the hour. As a parallel, some, like Aquinas (*Comp. Theo.* 242), note that God says to Abraham after the potential sacrifice of Isaac,

---

[66] See Archer (2017), Gaine (2015b, chap. 6), and Moloney (2000, 28–32) for additional discussion of these passages.

[67] For Cyril, see Bartel (1991, 35). For Augustine, see *De Trinitate* I.12.23. For Aquinas's reference to Chrysostom, see *ST* III q.10 a.2 *ad* 1. For Gregory, see Denzinger (2002, paragraph 248). For Maximus, see Moloney (2000, 46). For Aquinas's response, see his *Compendium of Theology*, 242. For Aquinas's discussions of Luke 2:52, see: *QDV* q.20 a.1 *sed contra*; *Comp. Theol.* 216; *ST* III q.7 a.12 *obj* 3 and ad 3; *ST* III q.12 a.2 *sed contra*, *resp*, and *ad* 3; his Commentary on John, 1:14, no. 264. For a critical discussion of Aquinas's approach, see Maritain (1969, 50–54).

"Now I know that you fear God" (Gen. 22:12). Aquinas argues that this does not mean that God went from ignorance to knowing that Abraham feared him. Rather, God was declaring it *made known* that Abraham feared him.

6.2.2 Christ's Knowledge and Freedom

Supposing that Christ had knowledge by means of his human intellect of all future contingent states – a view Aquinas claimed was held by everyone (Aquinas 1954, *QDV* q.8 a.4 resp) – difficulties arise concerning freedom, both his and ours.

Concerning our freedom, some of the most common responses to the problem of foreknowledge and freedom fail to generalize if Christ had such knowledge. For instance, open theism, the view that the future is open and so not knowable, fails as a solution. It fails because, on supposition, Christ *does* know the future. In addition, the Eternity Solution, the view that God knows things atemporally and so does not know them as *fore*knowledge, fails as well. For even if the divine knowledge is atemporal, Christ's infused human knowledge is in the past.[68] A third potential response to this problem is to understand our freedom as consistent with determinism, as the Compatibilists do. On such a view, deriving that we couldn't do otherwise than what we do at any time wouldn't imply our lack of freedom. A fourth response is to note that Christ's infused knowledge is of the same type as our knowledge. But what we know is made to be true by how the world is, not vice versa. So likewise, Christ's human knowledge is explained by how the world is, not vice versa. You have control over Christ's past human knowledge, insofar as you have control over what you do, and it is *because of* what you do that Christ knows what he knows, not vice versa.[69]

Concerning Christ's freedom, there are three problems to consider. First is the issue of whether the beatific vision removes freedom, insofar as, traditionally conceived, it prohibits the choice of sin in the blessed in heaven. Is Christ's freedom thus constrained by his beatific knowledge? Provided that there is at least one account of the freedom of the redeemed whereby they have the beatific vision, are free, and cannot sin, this objection will fail. Such accounts appear in the contemporary philosophical literature.[70]

Second, one might think that freedom requires deliberation, but that someone with perfect knowledge of what he *will* do cannot deliberate about his future

---

[68] For more on this point, see Pawl (2019b, chap. 7). For recent discussions of the Eternity Solution, see Cobreros (2016), Leftow (1991; 2009), Rota (2010), Stump and Kretzmann (1981; 1991), and Zagzebski (1991). For recent discussions of open theism, see Hasker (1998), Oord, Hasker and Zimmerman (2011), Rhoda (2007; 2008; 2011), Sanders (1998), and Tuggy (2007).

[69] To see this response worked out in more detail, see Pawl (2019b, chap. 7)

[70] For more on the freedom of the blessed in heaven, see Brown (2015), Cowan (2011), Henderson (2014; 2016), Pawl and Timpe (2009; 2013; 2016; 2017), and Tamburro (2014).

actions. No one can take as a deliberative option something he is positive he will not do. And Christ is positive that he will not do anything but exactly what he does. So he has no alternative deliberative options. So he cannot deliberate. So he is not free. Does foreknowledge ruin deliberation and so ruin freedom? In response, one might deny that deliberation is required for all acts of freedom. Rather, deliberation is required for cases of ignorance about what one ought to do. Christ does not fulfill that condition. So he need not deliberate to be free.[71]

Third, it is impossible for explanation to be symmetric – that is, A can't explain B and also B explain A. But, if Christ knew the future, it would be at least possible for him to look to that future knowledge to determine what to do. That is, he could reason, "I know I act perfectly always, and so I can look forward to what I will do to see what I should do in this situation." If that were even possible, then it would be possible for his future knowledge to explain his past actions. But his past actions explain his future knowledge. So it would be possible for explanation to be symmetric – for his knowledge of his future actions to explain his past acting (given foreknowledge), and for his past acting to explain his knowledge of his future actions (since reality grounds truth). Thus, his foreknowledge of his own future actions implies that something impossible (symmetric explanation) is possible. That's contradictory. So he must not have foreknowledge of his own future actions. In response, one can distinguish types of explanation. True, no two things can explain each other *in the same way*. But if Christ's knowledge of his future actions is explanatorily prior in a *motivational* sense to his act, and his acting is explanatorily prior in a *grounding the truth of* sense, then we do not have a vicious explanatory circle here.[72]

6.3 Death and Descent

Many activities of Christ have not received careful attention in contemporary philosophy of religion or analytic theology, for instance, his dual nativities, as Second Constantinople refers to them (from the Father, and from Mary), his miracles, his resurrection, his ascension, his two energies (as Third Constantinople defines), etc. Two activities that have received some attention are his death and his descent into hell. As such, this section focuses on those two events.

How does one explain, ontologically speaking, what happens in Christ's death? The standard scholastic answer runs as follows. Christ had both a soul and a body. At death, his soul and his body separated, but the component parts of his human nature remained united to the divine nature, though not to each other. In virtue of that remaining union of the parts of the human nature to the divine

---

[71] For a discussion of the problem of deliberation, see Pawl (2014c; 2019b, chap. 8).

[72] For more discussion of the problem of explanatory priority, see Pawl (2014b; 2019b, chap. 8).

nature, that which the component parts undergo can still rightly be said of Christ. So, for instance, it is true that he was buried, since his human body was buried. And it is true that he descended into hell, at least on these medieval accounts and on the traditional view of the earlier theologians, since his human soul descended into hell. At the resurrection, those parts of the human nature were knit together again, and so Christ was an integrated human being again thereafter.[73]

6.4 Conclusion

This section has charted the current discussions on the activities of Christ in analytic philosophy of religion. As noted, various areas remain underdeveloped in these literatures. The main areas of discussion concern Christ's knowing, willing, and death. On the traditional view, he was free with respect to both wills, though he could not sin. Traditionally, he knew everything with the divine intellect and all created things with his human intellect, though this did not negatively affect his freedom or ours. His death has traditionally been explained as the separation of his body and soul, and his resurrection explained as their being rejoined.

7 The Fundamental Philosophical Problem

The doctrine of the Incarnation faces an objection of obvious, odious contradiction. For, as found in the writings stemming from the ecumenical councils and in the work of many of the most influential Christian theologians, it affirms apparently contradictory predicates of Christ. As Richard Cross puts the objection:

> [T]he fundamental philosophical problem specific to the doctrine is this: how is it that one and the same thing could be both divine (and thus, on the face of it, necessary, and necessarily omniscient, omnipotent, eternal, immutable, impassible, and impeccable) and human (and thus, on the face of it, have the complements of all these properties)? (Cross 2011, 453)

Christ is immutable and mutable, impassible and passible, filling all creation and located at the bosom of Mary, etc. How could one make sense of such claims?[74]

---

[73] For current discussion on this issue, see Jaeger (2017), Jaeger and Sienkiewicz (2018), Nevitt (2016), and Turner (2017; 2019).

[74] A brief sampling of other discussions of this problem includes: Adams (2006, 121–123; 2009, 242–243), Arcadi (2018), Davis (2006, 116), Dawson (2004, 161–162), Evans (2006a, 13), Feenstra (2006, 142–144), Gordon (2016, 64), Gorman (2000a; 2011; 2014; 2016; 2017, chap. 6), Hebblethwaite (2008, 60), Hick (1989, 415; 2006, 66–70), Hill (2012, 3), Kelly (1994), Klima (1984), Labooy (2019), Leftow (2011, 316), Le Poidevin (2009b, 704), Loke (2009, 51; 2011, 493–494), Macquarrie (1990), Moreland and Craig (2003, 597), Morris (1987,

7.1 A Statement of the Problem

Focusing on just one instance of the problem, we can state it this way:[75]

1. Anything divine is impassible.   (assume)
2. Anything human is passible.   (assume)
3. Nothing can be both passible and impassible.   (assume)
4. Christ is divine and human.   (orthodox Christology)
5. Christ is both passible and impassible.   (from 1, 2, 4)
6. Contradiction! (from 3, 5)

We have seen in previous sections that 4 is a requirement of Conciliar Christology. For just one example, the Nicene Creed states that Jesus Christ is both God and human; he is "true god" and "became human" (Tanner 1990, 5). In Section 3, we have seen that the Christology of the ecumenical councils affirms Christ's impassibility. We've seen in Sections 2 and 4 the need for claiming that Christ was passible. He suffered at the hands of others, after all. And even if the evidence in Sections 2, 3, and 4 is insufficient to show that *anything* human is passible or *anything* divine is impassible, the premises themselves are stronger than we need. We only need the premises that Christ himself is impassible and passible.

The proponent of orthodox Christology has reason to accept 1, 2, and 4 from the conciliar texts. Even if there's some reason to deny 1 or 2, there's still independent reason to accept Sub-conclusion 5. For just a brief summary of reasons from influential theologians and conciliar texts, consider the following. Athanasius says "that Christ 'suffered and did not suffer'" (Anatolios 2004, 70). Aquinas approvingly quotes John of Damascus:

> All the properties of the human, just as of the Divine Nature, may be predicated equally of Christ. Hence Damascene says (De Fide Orth. iii, 4) that "Christ Who [is] God and Man, is called created and uncreated, passible and impassible." (*ST* III q.16 a.8 ad.2)

Finally, and perhaps most forcefully for those interested in affirming the orthodox faith concerning the Incarnation, the Fourth Council of Constantinople says of the seventh ecumenical council:

> We also know that the seventh, holy and universal synod, held for the second time at Nicaea, taught correctly when it professed the one and same Christ as both invisible and visible lord, incomprehensible and comprehensible,

---

chap. 1; 2009), Pawl (2014a; 2015; 2016b; 2016d, chaps. 4–7; 2018), Riches (2016, 5, 166), Senor (2002, 221), Spence (2008, 16), Stump (1989; 2004; 2005, chap. 14), Sturch (1991, chaps. 2, 12), Vallicella (2002), Van Inwagen (1998, secs. 2–4), and Wellum (2016, 446–455).

[75] Here I present the argument as I did in Pawl (2015) and summarize the findings from that article and from chapters 4–7 of Pawl (2016).

unlimited and limited, incapable and capable of suffering [*impassibilem etiam et passibilem*], inexpressible and expressible in writing. (Tanner 1990, 162)

Conciliar Christology requires the affirmation of apparently inconsistent predicates of Christ. That said, not everyone who discusses the Fundamental Problem feels bound to the conciliar texts. As such, a variety of solutions exists to this problem, some consistent with the conciliar texts, some not. In the remainder of this section, I discuss responses to this problem with an eye to which premise they deny.

7.2 Response 1: Revise Standard Logic

Such a response might go in two ways.[76] One might reject the validity of some inference forms, or one might reject the standard notion of identity, opting instead for *relative identity*.

7.2.1 Reject Classical Logic

The rejection of classical logic subdivides, depending on whether the rejected inference forms are meant to curtail the derivation of a contradiction, or whether they are meant to stop the spread of contradictions that are accepted. Along the first divide, one might accept the premises, but reject the universality of some inference form that allows the conclusion of a contradiction in the first place. Along the second, one might accept the truth of the contradictory conclusion, but reject the rules required for the contradiction to spread and ruin everything (this is sometimes called *explosion*, with good reason). I discuss each in turn here.

First, one might accept the claims of the argument but reject some inference to the contradiction, either the inference to 5 or the final inference to 6. For instance, Martin Luther (1971, 256) writes in a disputation that "there are syllogisms that are valid in logic, but not in theology." Such a move, if viable, would allow him to avoid the derivation of a contradiction at the cost of rejecting the universality of some common inference rules (Cf. Dahms 1978, 375).

Second, one might accept the conclusion, but reject the problematic consequences by limiting the entailment relations allowed in the Christological domain of discourse. Yes, Christ has both complementary predicates apt of him. What we have here is a contradiction. It is true that a proposition is true and that very same proposition, at the very same time, in the very same respect, is

---

[76] Let "standard logic" name classical logic plus an absolute identity relation.

false. But logic is such that we cannot derive from that contradiction just anything. This view rejects the validity of the Law of the Excluded Middle. Such a response allows the contradiction but precludes the spread of the contradiction. The work of Jc Beall (2019) is the best place to look for this strategy.[77]

7.2.2 Accept Relative Identity

The relative identity strategy contends that some – often all – identity claims are incomplete without a *sortal*, a type, under which the two things are identical. "Clark Kent is Superman" is an incomplete claim it is similar to "Edith is to the left of." What is needed in each case is another term: Clark is *the same person as* Superman; Edith is to the left of *Agnes*. Importantly for the relative identity theorist, two things can be the same x without being the same y. In addition, as Peter van Inwagen (1998) shows, Leibniz's Law fails if relative identity is true. That is, A and B can be the same x and A have a feature without B having that feature. This is relevant to the Fundamental Problem, since the human-natured thing can be possible, and the human-natured thing can be the same person as the divine-natured thing, without the divine-natured thing being possible. Thus, the inference to 5, which says that one and the same thing is both possible and impossible, is fallacious, given relative identity. Some people claim that relative identity is necessary for the doctrine of the Trinity – the Father and the Son are *the same God*, but they are not *the same person.*[78] If this is so, then by accepting the relative identity solution here the Christian does not incur any additional costs, as they will already have been paid for the doctrine of the Trinity.[79]

7.2.3 The Traditional Assumption of Standard Logic

The vast majority of theological authors accept the classical entailment relations, as we can see from their discussions of their opponents' views. Very often the giants of theological discourse argue against their opponents by pointing out the entailments of their views, then reasoning that, since these entailments are false, the opponents' views must be as well. Such argumentation requires the

---

[77] I discuss this strategy and objections to it in more detail in Pawl (2019a). I thank Beall for his helpful discussion on this strategy.

[78] The logic of this solution is difficult. To see it worked out carefully, see Baber (2015; 2016; 2019), Conn (2012), and Jedwab (2015; 2018). To see some objections to relative identity in a Trinitarian context, see Rea (2003).

[79] My thanks to Joseph Jedwab for his patient help in understanding the relative identity response to the Fundamental Problem.

use of some inference forms that Luther and Beall (for different reasons) would want to preclude from the Christological domain.

In what follows, I employ classical logic. I again point the reader to the work of Beall (2019), though, to see how one could answer the Fundamental Problem by revising logic (or, perhaps as he would say, by realizing the proper extent of logic). I also assume an absolute identity relation.

7.3 Response 2: Deny Some Predicates of Christ

On the assumption of classical logic, no one should affirm a contradiction. So, everyone, friend or foe of Conciliar Christology, will need to deny some premise of the argument given in Section 7.1. One can deny the relevant predicates of Christ in at least four ways. One could (1) categorically deny all the divine predicates, (2) categorically deny all the human predicates, (3) categorically deny some mixture of predicates, such that one predicate from each allegedly contradictory pair is denied, or (4) deny some mixture of the predicates at some time or other, such that one predicate from each pair is denied for all times, though not necessarily the same predicate at each time.

7.3.1 Deny All Divine Predicates

The proponent of the view under discussion here denies that Christ is divine, and so denies 4, and is thus not required to affirm 5 or the contradictory 6.

Someone with such a view could affirm that Christ is a mere human, perhaps a charlatan who deceived his disciples. Or Christ could still be an important divine messenger, yet a messenger that is not God – at least not God in the sense meant in traditional Christian doctrine, and so need not have the divine attributes. In either case, the councils are massively wrong in the orthodox teaching concerning Christ. One finds this view – that Christ has a special theological status but is not God – discussed under the title "Arianism" in the early church. This view, while it resolves the contradiction, is inconsistent with Conciliar Christology, insofar as Conciliar Christology requires the divinity of the God-man.[80]

7.3.2 Deny All Human Predicates

The logic of this maneuver is similar to the logic of the previous response. Such a thinker denies 4, due to denying the second conjunct, that Christ is human. If all specifically human predicates are denied, then "human" is denied of Christ, and so the second conjunct of Premise 4 is false. In such a case, Christ only

---

[80] See Hick (2006) for more on this approach.

appeared to have the human attributes. He only appeared to be passible, for instance.

Such a view, so far as I know, has no current or even recent defenders in the philosophical discussions of the Incarnation (in fact, even calling it an *Incarnation* is faulty on this view). One finds this view – that Christ only appeared to become human – discussed under the title "Docetism" (see Section 4.2.1). This view is inconsistent with Conciliar Christology, insofar as Conciliar Christology requires the humanity of the God-man.

7.3.3 Deny Some Mixture of Predicates at All Times

This type of response has many advocates today. The idea can be pictured as follows. One can make a list of all of the pairs of allegedly contradictory attributes that a God-man would have. Then, one goes through each pair, crossing off one or the other of the two attributes, such that no pair has both predicates left at the end of the excising. For instance, perhaps God need not be impassible. Thus, Premise 1 is false. In another case, perhaps humans need not really be limited in power, and so the Fundamental Problem constructed with "omnipotent" and "limited in power" as the allegedly contradictory pair has a false second premise. And so on. For every pair, at least one of the attributes fails to be implied by being divine or by being human.

Scholars can use two main methods, always in tandem, to work this strategy. (To do either alone would be to fall back into the previous two strategies discussed.) The first is to weaken or eliminate some of the divine attributes associated with classical theism. On such a view, it is false that God must be impassible, immutable, eternal, and simple (or false that God is any of these ways in a robust, problematic sense), and so any form of the Fundamental Problem that includes those attributes has a false first premise.

The second step is to make a distinction going back at least to St. John of Damascus (676–749), but more recently revitalized by Thomas Morris. The Damascene writes:

> The whole He, then is perfect God, but not exclusively God, because He is not only God but also man. Likewise, the whole He is perfect man, but not exclusively man, because He is not only man but also God.[81]

Morris (1987, 65–67) makes the same distinction with the terms *merely* (for exclusively) and *fully* (for perfect). Armed with this distinction, one turns to the Fundamental Problem with an eye toward distinguishing the second premise. Yes, the responder says, it is true that anything *merely* human is, say, limited in

---

[81] This quotation is taken, with slight modification, from John of Damascus (2000, 283).

knowledge or power. But, the responder continues, it is false that anything *fully* human is limited in knowledge or power. Similarly, it is true that anything *merely* divine is impassible, but false that anything *fully* divine is impassible. Of course, it is the *fully* claim that the objector needs for this argument to apply to Christ. After all, the *merely* interpretation of the premise would itself preclude the truth of Premise 4, that Christ is both God and human – being *merely* human implies not being both human *and divine*. Were the proponent of the Fundamental Problem to employ the *merely* premise, the argument's premises would contradict one another, and so the argument would be unsound.

To summarize: consider the cases of the Fundamental Problem in which one means to excise the human predicate. Armed with the distinction between *merely* human and *fully* human, those instances of the Fundamental Problem can be put in two ways, depending on how one understands the second premise. On the *merely* reading, the truth of the second premise contradicts the truth of the fourth premise, and so the argument is unsound. On the *fully* reading, this response claims that the second premise is false, and so the argument is unsound. Thus, the argument is unsound.

What to make of this strategy? In the end, even if there were a consistent, uniform manner of applying this strategy in solving the Fundamental Problem, there's still the fact that such a move leaves the contradiction in place for many who affirm the doctrine of the Incarnation. Very many defenders of the Incarnation take it as a given that the texts cited in Section 7.1, in which Christ is predicated by apparently incompatible predicates, as well as many other texts from the councils and theologians, are to be believed. So, even if there were grounds for denying Premise 1 or Premise 2 for each presentation of the Fundamental Problem, the traditional texts preclude simply ruling out the apparently incompatible predications of Christ. Christ must remain both passible and impassible, for instance, on this view. Assuming the truth of Premise 3, which this solution does nothing to challenge, the proponent of traditional Christianity still faces a contradiction. For this large swath of past and present proponents of the Incarnation, one must look elsewhere for a reply.

In addition, some varieties of this solution appear to collapse into the following solution (Section 7.3.4). To see why, consider the Word pre-Incarnation. He is then both merely and fully divine, and so, on this response, he is impassible (since "anything *merely* divine is impassible" is conceded on this view). Once incarnate, he is fully but not merely divine. Once incarnate, he is not impassible – were he still impassible, we would not have avoided his being both passible and impassible in the incarnation, and so this view would not have resolved the contradiction. Thus, this solution looks to require the predications concerning Christ to change their truth value at different times, as the next solution claims.

7.3.4 Deny Different Predicates at Different Times

Suppose one wanted to accept that Christ had both of the apparently incompatible attributes. How might one go about doing so? One might claim he had them, but not *at the same time* or *in the same respect*. Or, one might deny their incompatibility *full stop*, even at the same time in the same respect. This section canvasses each option, starting in this section with the claim that Christ had the apparently incompatible predicates, but not at the same time.

The kenotic view takes its lead from a passage of Scripture.[82] Paul writes in Philippians 2:6–8 that Christ:

> who, though he was in the form of God, did not regard equality
>   with God as something to be exploited,
> but emptied himself, taking the form of a slave, being born in
>   human likeness. And being found in human form,
> he humbled himself and became obedient to the point of death –
>   even death on a cross. *(NRSV)*

This self-emptying – *kenosis* – is the impetus for the kenotic view. While kenotic Christology ought not to be seen as merely a response to the Fundamental Problem, it has been used as one such response, in the following way.

It is true, says the kenotic opponent of the Fundamental Problem, that anything that is divine is immutable or impassible *at some point*. And true, anything human is limited in knowledge and power *at some point*. But, importantly, these might not be the same times. And, if not the same times, then Christ's being impassible and passible or being omnipotent and limited in power are no more contradictory than your being seated at one time and standing at another. What the Fundamental Problem would have to show, and what its kenotic opponent would fight hard to deny, is that Christ must have both attributes *at the same time*. In summary: the first two premises need an "at some time" modifier added to them, and the last three lines of the Fundamental Problem need "at the same time" modifiers added to them. Once the temporal modification is made explicit, the contradiction is no longer derivable.

This theory faces some objections. First, is there a time at which Christ is both incarnate and no longer self-emptying? Many have claimed there is. The doctrine of the *exaltation* claims that after his resurrection, Christ is glorified

---

[82] For more on kenosis, see Archer (2017), Crisp (2007b, chap. 5), Davis (2011), Evans (2006a), Feenstra (2006), Le Poidevin (2009b, sec. 6; 2013), Senor (2011), and Thompson (2006).

to his rightful place, bearing all his divine majesty and attributes. At that point, Christ is still human, yet he is exalted to his former status. If the doctrine of the exaltation is true, then kenotic Christology will not provide a universal answer to the Fundamental Problem. For there will be some time, any post-exaltation time, at which Christ has all the attributes humans must have in addition to the attributes of which he supposedly emptied during his earthly mission.[83]

Second, depending on how one understands kenotic Christology, it can appear inconsistent with Conciliar Christology.[84] For the conciliar texts teach that Christ, even when incarnate, retained the very divine attributes kenotic thinkers look to deny of him during his Incarnation. Cyril writes of Christ that, while a baby, "he filled the whole of creation and was fellow ruler with him who begot him" (Tanner 1990, 51). And Leo, discussing the very text from Philippians 2, says that "that self-emptying whereby the invisible rendered himself visible, and the Creator and Lord of all things chose to join the ranks of mortals, spelled no failure of power" (Tanner 1990, 78). Christ's power is not diminished, according to Leo, even though he becomes a baby. This teaching – that Christ, even while united completely to the human nature in the Incarnation, remained with the Father in heaven, ruling all of creation – was given the pejorative name the *extra calvinisticum* (roughly, "that extra thing Calvin added"), in later Protestant polemics.[85]

7.4 Response 3: "Qua" Responses

The previous section, 7.3.4, focused on a response to the Fundamental Problem that granted the incompatibility of the predicates in question (e.g., impassible and passible) when had *at the same time* and *in the same respect*, but it denied that the predicates were apt at the same time. This section focuses on a family of strategies that accepts that Christ was both, for instance, passible and impassible, at the same time, but denies that he was both *in the same respect*, and so denies the actual incompatibility.

Put in terms of the argument presented in Section 7.1, this strategy, as the previous one, claims that Premise 3 is incompletely stated. It should state that nothing can be both passible and impassible at the same time, *in the same respect*. To derive a contradiction, then, Sub-conclusion 5 would have to say that Christ is passible and impassible at the same time, *in the same respect* (henceforth, I drop the "at the same time" clause, as it is not germane to this

---

[83] For a more in-depth discussion of kenoticism and the exaltation, see Evans (2006b, 200–202), Feenstra (1989, 144–149), and Pawl (2016d, 114–115).

[84] For this argumentation spelled out in more detail, see Pawl (2016d, chap. 5, sect V.b.).

[85] For the history of the use of the term, see Willis (1966, 8–25). For more recent work on the *extra calvinisticum*, see Gordon (2016) and McGinnis (2014).

response to the argument). The proponent of this solution denies Sub-conclusion 5 so revised. How?

A common mode of speech, found in the ecumenical councils, says that Christ is one way *according to his human nature* and an apparently incompatible way *according to his divine nature*. For instance, Christ is impassible *according to his divinity* and is passible *according to his humanity*. This "according to" phrase is often left untranslated as "qua." So, for instance, Christ, qua human, is limited in space, but Christ, qua divine, is omnipresent. Moreover, it is false that Christ, qua human, is omnipresent, and it is false that Christ, qua divine, is limited in space. As such, the revised Sub-conclusion 5, which requires that Christ be passible and impassible *in the same respect*, is false. What to make of this solution to the Fundamental Problem?

It is a good opening move in response to the Fundamental Problem, but, spelled out only this far, it is unsatisfactory. An analogy will make the unsatisfactory nature of the response clear. Suppose that I told you that, against every prior expectation, I had succeeded in drawing a shape that is both a square and a circle.[86] You would be rightly incredulous. You'd likely say something like the following:

> A necessary condition for being a circle is that the shape have all its points equidistant from a center point. And a necessary condition for being a square is that the shape have four 90-degree angles and four straight lines of equal length. No one shape can fulfill both those necessary conditions. So no one shape can be both a square and a circle. You must be mistaken.

Now, suppose I responded to you by noting that you're right concerning the necessary conditions. Nothing can have those features *in the same respect*. But you've overlooked that the shape I've drawn has all its points equidistant from a center point *according to its circularity*, or qua circle, and that it has four straight lines and four 90-degree angles *according to its squareness*, or qua square.

Are all your worries now alleviated? Likely not. In fact, now we have additional quandaries. What does it mean for one single shape to have inconsistent features in these different respects? If we were to look at it, would we see four angles or not? Without further analysis, this method of solution to both the Fundamental Problem and the Square Circle Problem (as we might call it) is incomplete and unhelpful. It is no surprise, then, that contemporary

---

[86] Here I borrow an analogy Hick (1977, 178) makes concerning the coherence of orthodox Christology. See also the clever work of Angere (2017), though, who argues that there can be square circles, and, in fact, that it is "quite likely that there are square circles in the universe" (88). Angere includes a figure, Figure 4, on page 86, which shows a square circle (note: it looks like a square and not like a circle).

authors who consider this solution often charge it with "muddying the waters" (Morris 1987, 49).[87]

For this reason, it behooves the proponent of this strategy to say more about what exactly the "qua human" or "qua divine" modifier is doing in the solution. Elsewhere I've distinguished four things the "qua" might be doing, then subdivided two of them, for a total of six qua strategies.[88] Here I add a seventh "qua" strategy. There is no space in this Element to provide a complete treatment of these strategies (for that, look at chapter 6 of Pawl (2016d), which itself is two-thirds the length of the body of this Element). Here we must be content with a brief summary of the strategies.

Most generally, the strategies can be distinguished by what the "qua" modifies. It could modify the whole of the assertion or a part. If just a part, then, since there are three parts – "Christ," "is," "(im)passible" – there are three ways to modify a part with the "qua." It could modify the subject of the assertion ("Christ-qua-divine"), the copula ("is-qua-divine"), or the predicate ("[im]passible-qua-divine").[89] The remainder of this section discusses each of these options. While each option modifies something different, the argumentative goal is the same. The goal is to revise Premises 3 and 5, claiming that, understood in the same sense, they are not both true. That is, they all aim to replace 3 and 5 with the following:

3*. Nothing can be both passible and impassible *in the same respect.*
5*. Christ is both passible and impassible *in the same respect.*

3* and 5* are together contradictory. Each qua theory discussed in what follows provides some way to deny 5*, and so to deny that a contradiction has been derived.

7.4.1 Modifying the Assertion

This first understanding of the "qua" modifier takes it to modify the whole assertion: Qua divine, Christ is impassible. The "qua" clause serves to point out that in virtue of which the subject has the predicate. It is because Christ is divine that he is impassible.

Scholars have rightly criticized this understanding in the literature. For if something is a certain way because it is another – if S is P because it is N – then it follows that S is P. If I am warm-blooded because I am human, then I am warm-

---

[87] See also Van Inwagen (1998, sec. 4) and Holland (2012, 74) for criticisms of the qua move.

[88] See Pawl (2015; 2016b; 2016b, chap. 6).

[89] For more on divisions of qua clauses, see Adams (2009), Bäck (1997; 2008, 84–87), Cross (2005, 193–199; 2011, 455–456), Labooy (2019), Morris (1987, 48–49), and Senor (2002, 229–33).

blooded. But then, we haven't avoided the contradiction between Premises 3 and 5 after all. The qua-modified assertion implies the non-qua-modified assertion with which we started. Those non-qua-modified assertions, though, the qua-strategist grants, cannot be true of the same thing at the same time. Since, on this strategy, the qua modification that was intended to get the predicates apt of Christ *in different respects* collapses back into the non-qua-modified, problematic claims, we are no closer to solving the Fundamental Problem.

A novel understanding of modifying the assertion, one that does not fall prey to the previous objection, has recently been put forward by Beall and Henderson (2019). Their view takes seriously the prima facie fact that the qua locutions are sentential operators, modifying the assertion into a different assertion. On this view, the qua modifiers serve to designate in which "story" about Christ the qua-modified propositions are true. It is true *in the divine story* that Christ is impassible, but true *in the human story* that he is passible. And, importantly, stories cannot be combined (they call it "unionized" [2019, 160]) into a single, larger story. The truth of "Christ is impassible in the divine story" does not, on this view, imply that "Christ is impassible" *full stop*; S is P qua N *does not imply* S is P. And one cannot derive from "S is P qua N1" and "S is not-P qua N2" that "S is P and not-P." Thus, one cannot derive 6. Instead, one derives Christ is impassible in the divine story and Christ is passible in the human story. That is not contradictory, according to this solution.

This solution has some costs. It requires that unionizing true stories about the same individual is not universally valid. It requires that it is not universally valid to derive a true, qua-unadorned statement about a person from a true story about that person. And it requires that both "Christ is impassible" is not true and "Christ is not impassible" is not true (Beall and Henderson 2019, 166). These considerations are not news to the authors, who carefully consider nine objections to the view in their article, including some of these objections.

7.4.2 Modifying the Subject

The second understanding of the "qua" modifier takes it to modify the subject: Christ-qua-divine is impassible. The "qua" serves to disambiguate the subject of the predicate. It is Christ-qua-divine that is impassible; it is Christ-qua-human that is passible. Which premise or inference of the Fundamental Problem would the proponent of this strategy challenge? Again, it would revise Premise 3 to include an *in the same respect* clause, and it would say that Premise 5 is false – Christ, the one person, is not both passible and impassible *in the same respect*.

The thing, Christ-qua-human, is possible; the thing, Christ-qua-divine, is impassible.

To see the problems with this view, consider the relations between the subjects of the predications so far discussed: Christ, Christ-qua-divine, and Christ-qua-human. Are any of these three identical with one another? Either they are identical or they are not. What follows is a proof by cases.

Suppose that they all name the same entity. At least two problems arise. First, if a and b are identical, anything true of a is true of b and vice versa.[90] So, if Christ-qua-divine is identical to Christ-qua-human, then, since Christ-qua-divine is impassible, it follows that Christ-qua-human is impassible. But that's false – Christ-qua-human is not impassible.

Second, if they are all identical (in the nonrelativistic sense), then this solution does not solve the contradiction after all. This solution is premised on the acceptance of the two attributes being incompatible when said of the same thing at the same time in the same respect. And it attempted to resolve the Fundamental Problem by noting that these predicates were not said in the same respect, since, *really*, they were not said of the same thing. But then, if the next move were to identify the subjects, subjects differentiated to avoid contradiction, then we haven't made any headway in solving the Fundamental Problem. I think the strategy must therefore require some real distinction between at least two of the subjects discussed.

Suppose, then, for the other case in our proof by cases, that there are at least two separate entities among the three. In such a case, perhaps one could stop both allegedly contradictory predicates from spreading to one subject. Here too the view faces problems.

First, it seems contrary to the Communication of Idioms (see Section 5.2). Christ's human nature exists in a manner that would typically make a person with a human nature be passible. And his divine nature exists in a manner that would typically make a person with that divine nature be impassible. The Communication of Idioms would imply that the one person is both passible and impassible, then. But this view must deny that implication on pain of reinstating the contradiction.

Second, this view sits poorly with Conciliar Christology, which requires both the divine and human attributes to be said of one and the same person. As just one instance of many, Cyril says in his third letter to Nestorius, "in thinking rightly, we refer both the human and divine expressions to the same person" (Tanner 1990, 55). If this qua strategy were to allow the predication of both

---

[90] The conditional in this sentence is sometimes referred to as *Leibniz's Law*. To see a response that rejects the use of Leibniz's Law, see the relative identity response in Section 7.2.2.

expressions to the one person, it would have no means by which to claim that the (allegedly) contradictory predicates do not imply a contradiction.[91]

7.4.3 Modifying the Copula

The third understanding of the "qua" modifier takes it to modify the copula of the assertion: Christ is-qua-divine impassible, or, put otherwise, Christ is-divinely impassible.[92] The "qua" serves to disambiguate the different copulas involved in the assertions. The opponent of the Fundamental Problem who prefers this strategy will claim that while it is true that the predicates cannot be apt of Christ at the same time in the same respect, it is false that they are apt of Christ in the same respect, and so Premise 5, when revised as 5*, is false. Christ is-divinely impassible and the very same Christ is-humanly passible.

This strategy for answering the Fundamental Problem can be subdivided in two ways. It could be that there are different copulas – is-divinely, is-humanly, is-bovinely, etc. – for each kind of thing that there is. Or, it could be that there is only a single copula with a variable built into it – is-$x$ly – and the difference between the Christological claims comes down to what one substitutes in for x. Since the latter includes a variable for which one can substitute in nature types, we can call that the *substitutional copula* view. Since the former includes no variables, but rather a plethora of different copulas, we can call that the *non-substitutional copula* view.[93] Consider each.

The non-substitutional copula view requires multiple copulas, minimally, is-divinely and is-humanly. Limiting the number of copulas to two, though, would imply that we couldn't say anything about anything aside from humans and the divine. "Fido is a dog" is true, but that "is" cannot be the divine or human copula. It seems, then, that for any type of thing, there must be a distinct copula for it. Is there, in addition to these narrow copulas, a universal copula as well? The non-substitutional theorist should deny the existence of a universal copula. For, were there such a thing, an inference from "Christ is-divinely impassible" to "Christ is impassible" would seem war-ranted. If it weren't, in what sense would the copula be *universal*? If one couldn't go from the particular to the universal copula, then, since everything is of some type, there would be no instance in which one could employ a universal copula. Far from being universal, then, it would be inapplicable. The substitutional copula view does have a universal copula, unlike the non-substitutional view.

---

[91] For a recent defense of the strategy of this section, see Labooy (2019).

[92] I discuss this qua strategy at length in Pawl (2016d, 143–150).

[93] I discuss these views in depth in Pawl (2016d, 143–150).

Both the substitutional view and the non-substitutional view, were they employed, have a shared cost. Each would require a modification in our standard logical formulation of arguments. For standard formulation of logic has no means of demarcating various copulas.

Additional adverbial solutions to the Fundamental Problem are rare in the contemporary discussion.[94] One instance of a different sort of adverbial solution comes from Bohn (2012), who distinguishes, not between humanly and divinely had predicates, but between merely, fundamentally, and essentially *true* propositions.

7.4.4 Modifying the Predicate

The fourth understanding of the "qua" modifier takes it to modify the predicate of the assertion: Christ is impassible-qua-divine.[95] The "qua" serves to disambiguate the different predicates involved in the assertions. The opponent of the Fundamental Problem who prefers this strategy will claim that while it is true that "passible" and "impassible" cannot be apt of Christ at the same time in the same respect, such is not what her Christology requires. Christ isn't both "passible" and "impassible"; Christ is "passible-qua-human" and "impassible-qua-divine." While "passible" and "impassible" are contradictories on this solution to the Fundamental Problem, there's no good reason to think that "passible-qua-human" and "impassible-qua-divine" are. Thus, this view of the predicates required of Christ does not predicate allegedly incompatible predicates of Christ. Again, Premise 5* of the Fundamental Problem is false.

This final "qua" strategy subdivides between a substitutional and a non-substitutional conception of the qua-relativized predicates. Are there various predicates – possible-qua-human, possible-qua-dog, possible-qua-cat, etc.? Or is there just one relational predicate – possible-qua-x, where one can substitute any kind term for x? Each version of the strategy has its own benefits and costs.

The non-substitutional qua modifying of the predicates yields some counterintuitive results. For instance, the word "animal" cannot be used univocally of both dogs and humans. For humans are *really* animals-qua-human, and dogs are *really* animals-qua-canine. And no human is anything qua-canine, neither is any dog anything qua-human. So there is no shared term to use here for both dogs and humans. That's surprising.

---

[94] Distinctions in ways of being are less rare, however. See, for instance, McDaniel (2017).
[95] I discuss this version of the qua strategy at length in Pawl (2016d, 129–143). See Gorman (2014; 2016; 2017, chap. 6) and Labooy (2019) for a recent sympathetic discussion of these "qua" clause strategies.

The proponent of the view under discussion here should fight the urge to reason as follows: "I am an animal-qua-human, so I am an animal *full stop*. Similar reasoning shows that Fido is an animal *full stop*. So, there *is* a shared term." Such reasoning – from the qua-modified predicate to the qua-unadorned predicate – would cause problems elsewhere. For, if generalized, we could do the same with the predicates correctly said of Christ, in which case we are back to passible and impassible being said of Christ *full stop* in the same respect.

A second problem the non-substitutional qua modifying of predicates faces are predicates that are not apt of Christ in virtue of either nature alone, as discussed in Section 5.2. For instance, Christ is "two-natured." But he is not two-natured-qua-human, and he isn't two-natured-qua-divine. How does one explain the qua modification of predicates here?

One thing that could be done is a restricting of which predicates get qua modified. Maybe *animal* and *two-natured* don't get modified. One hopes that the reasoning in determining which to modify is something more than merely cataloging the ones that cause problems, then labeling those as the modified ones. One would want a principle here, to safeguard against it being *ad hoc*.

The substitutional qua modifying of the predicates fares better with univocal predication across mundane cases. For both I and the dog are animal-qua-*something*. That something is different in each case, but the same predicate is apt of each of us. Similarly, parent-of-*someone* can be said of both me and many of my readers, even if it isn't the same someone in all but one case (that is, supposing that my wife ever reads this Element). The substitutionary qua modification of the predicates will still need some means by which to claim that Christ is *two-natured*, but not two-natured due to either nature alone. It will still require some principle for determining which predicates get modified and which do not.

7.5 Response 4: Revise the Truth Conditions of the Predicates in Question

Consider a final response. It accepts standard logic and the claim that Christ is, at the same time, and in the same respects, both passible and impassible, unlike all the other previous responses. It takes as its target Premise 3 (or 3*) of the argument: that nothing can be both passible and impassible at the same time, in the same respect.

If we understand passibility and impassibility as related to each other as logical complements – P and ~P – then it is clear that nothing can be both passible and impassible. For to be both would be to imply the truth of a contradiction, and we are supposing here that no contradictions are true. But what if they were related, not as contradictories, but as *subcontraries*? That is to say, what if they can both be apt of a thing, but it is false that they can both be inapt of a thing? I've presented the logic in detail elsewhere (Pawl 2014a; 2016d, chap. 7). Here I summarize it.

To see the distinction between contradictories and subcontraries, consider where the negation goes in the analysis of the predicate "impassible." Is to be impassible *not* to be able to be causally affected, with the negation on the outside, at the beginning of the analysis? Or does the negation go on the inside, for instance, by saying that to be impassible is to *have a nature that is not* able to be causally affected?[96] Understood in this second way, provided that one person has two natures, where one such nature can be causally affected and the other cannot be causally affected, then that one person can fulfill the conditions required for being both passible and impassible at the same time. Provided that everything has at least one nature (Christ alone, on traditional Christianity, has more than one), that nature will be either causally affectable or not. So everything will be either passible or impassible, and it is possible for one thing – a two-natured person – to be both. In other words, the predicates "passible" and "impassible" will be related as subcontraries, as defined in the previous paragraph. Is Christ passible? Yes; he has a nature that can be causally affected, and that's what's required to be passible. Is Christ impassible? Yes; he has a nature that cannot be causally affected, and that's what's required to be impassible. Both terms are truthfully predicated of the one person Jesus Christ.

In what sense are these terms said *in the same respect* of Christ? Well, "passible" is said in exactly the same way it is said of me. And "impassible" is said in exactly the same way it is said of the Holy Spirit. And neither I nor the Holy Spirit is both impassible and passible, owing to the fact that each of us has but one nature, and no one-natured thing could fulfill the conditions required for being both passible and impassible. Those two predicates would imply a contradiction were they both said of me. Given that they are contradictory when said of one-natured me, they must be said in the same respect of me. But they are said in those very same respects of Christ as they would be of me. So they are said in the same respect of Christ as well.

This view too faces some objections. It requires us to understand natures such that they can be causally affected. Such a notion of natures is contested. That

---

[96] This is an old distinction. Gabriel Biel (died 1495) used exactly this strategy to solve the Fundamental Problem; see Pawl (2019a, 442–447).

said, one finds such an understanding in the councils, where, as we saw in Section 4.1.3, Christ's human nature is said to hang on a cross.[97]

7.6 Conclusion

This section has discussed the Fundamental Problem of Christology – the question of how one thing could be both God and human, since, as God, he must have certain features, and, as human, have apparently contradictory features. For ease of explication, the section focused on one pair of features – impassibility and passibility – though the intent was to generalize to other features. The section canvassed four types of response, many subdivided further.

First, one might revise standard logic. This can be done by swapping absolute identity for relative identity. Or it can be done by rejecting the universal applicability of logical inference (as Luther does) or by accepting universal applicability but rejecting the validity of some classical inference forms, as Beall does.

Second, one might deny some of the worrisome predicates of Christ. Perhaps he isn't really impassible. Or perhaps he isn't really ignorant. Or perhaps he has both allegedly contradictory predicates apt of him, but he doesn't have them apt of him *at the same time*. In any case, this suite of strategies takes its defining feature to be denying some predicate of Christ, either at a time or categorically.

Third, one might accept standard logic, accept that the worrisome pairs of predicates are both apt (true) of Christ at the same time, but deny that they are true in the same respect. This move is typically made with the use of "qua" clauses. One must ask: how does the "qua" work? I provided four ways of understanding it. The "qua" clause could modify the whole assertion, modify the subject of the assertion, modify the copula, or modify the predicate. The first and last two methods further subdivide.

Fourth and finally, one might accept standard logic, accept the worrisome pairs of predicates are true of Christ at the same time, in the same respect, but deny that the worrisome predicate pairs are inconsistent. To do this, one could revise one's understanding of the predicate pairs so that they are subcontraries, each apt of a thing in virtue of some nature it has. Given that Christ has two natures, he (and only he, on traditional Christian doctrine) is in a position to satisfy both apparently contradictory predicates. Those predicates are inconsistent for all one-natured other things.

---

[97] For more on this robust notion of the human nature, see Pawl (2016d, 227–231; 2019b, 29–30; 2020).

Each method has its own costs and benefits, which I have only gestured toward here, while providing references to fuller discussions in the footnotes.

8 Conclusion

This Element has canvassed the current philosophical work on the doctrine of the Incarnation, the Christian view that God the Son assumed a human nature, and so became human. It focused on the metaphysical aspects of the traditional doctrine as espoused in the ecumenical councils of the first eight centuries of the Christian community, prior to the Great Schism.

The goal of this Element has been to present the content of Conciliar Christology, the main philosophical objection to that doctrine, and the most common responses to that objection. My hope is that the reader can use this information, along with the copious footnotes, to investigate the doctrine of the Incarnation more deeply.

References

Adams, Marilyn McCord. 1985. "The Metaphysics of the Incarnation in Some Fourteenth-Century Franciscans." In *Essays Honoring Allan B. Wolter*, edited by William A. Frank and Girard J. Etzkorn, 21–57. New York: Franciscan Institute.

1999. *What Sort of Human Nature? Medieval Philosophy and the Systematics of Christology*. Milwaukee, WI: Marquette University Press.

2000. *Horrendous Evils and the Goodness of God*. Ithaca, NY: Cornell University Press.

2004. "The Metaphysical Size Gap." *Sewanee Theological Review* 47 (2): 129–144.

2005. "What's Metaphysically Special about Supposits? Some Medieval Variations on Aristotelian Substance." *Aristotelian Society Supplementary Volume* 79 (1): 15–52.

2006. *Christ and Horrors: The Coherence of Christology*. 1st edition. Cambridge: Cambridge University Press.

2009. "Christ As God-Man, Metaphysically Construed." In *Oxford Readings in Philosophical Theology*, edited by Michael C. Rea, 239–263. Oxford: Oxford University Press.

de Aldama, SJ, Joseph A., and Iesu Solano, SJ. 2014. *Sacrae Theologiae Summa IIIA: On the Incarnate Word • On the Blessed Virgin Mary*. Translated by Kenneth Baker, SJ. 1st edition. Saddle River, NJ: Keep the Faith.

Alfeyev, Metropolitan Hilarion. 2012. *Orthodox Christianity: Doctrine and Teaching of the Orthodox Church*. Yonkers, NY: St. Vladimirs Seminary Press.

Anatolios, Khaled. 2004. *Athanasius*. New York: Routledge.

Angere, Staffan. 2017. "The Square Circle." *Metaphilosophy* 48 (1–2): 79–95. https://doi.org/10.1111/meta.12224.

Aquinas, Thomas. 1954. *The Disputed Questions on Truth (in Three Volumes)*. Translated by Robert Schmidt. Chicago: Regnery

2012. *Commentary on the Letter of Saint Paul to the Romans*. Translated by Fabian R. Larcher, John Mortensen, and Enrique Alarcón. Lander, WY: Aquinas Institute for the Study of Sacred Doctrine.

2013. *Commentary on the Gospel of Matthew 1–12*. Lander, WY: Aquinas Institute for the Study of Sacred Doctrine.

Arcadi, James M. 2018. "Recent Developments in Analytic Christology." *Philosophy Compass* 0 (0): e12480. https://doi.org/10.1111/phc3.12480.

Archer, Joel. 2017. "Kenosis, Omniscience, and the Anselmian Concept of Divinity." *Religious Studies*, March, 1–13. https://doi.org/10.1017/S0034412517000051.

Arendzen, J. P. 1941. *Whom Do You Say-?: A Study in the Doctrine of the Incarnation*. New York: Sheed and Ward.

Baber, H. E. 2015. "The Trinity." *Faith and Philosophy* 32 (2): 161–171. https://doi.org/10.5840/faithphil201541336.

    2016. "Trinity, Generality, and Dominance." *Religious Studies* 52 (4): 435–449. https://doi.org/10.1017/S003441251500058X.

    2019. *The Trinity: A Philosophical Investigation*. London: Scm Press.

Bäck, Allan T. 1997. *On Reduplication: Logical Theories of Qualification* (Studien Und Texte Zur Geistesgeschichte Des Mittelalters, No 49). Leiden: Brill.

    2008. "Aquinas on the Incarnation." *The New Scholasticism* 56 (2): 127–145.

Baker, Kenneth. 2013. *Jesus Christ – True God and True Man: A Handbook on Christology for Non-theologians*. South Bend, IN: Saint Augustine's Press.

Bartel, T. W. 1991. "Like Us in All Things, Apart from Sin?" *Journal of Philosophical Research* 16: 19–52.

    1995. "Why the Philosophical Problems of Chalcedonian Christology Have Not Gone Away." *Heythrop Journal* 36 (2): 153–172.

Bavinck, Herman. 2006. *Reformed Dogmatics, Vol. 3: Sin and Salvation in Christ*. Grand Rapids, MI: Baker Academic.

Beall, Jc. 2019. "Christ – A Contradiction: A Defense of Contradictory Christology." *Journal of Analytic Theology* 7: 400–433.

Beall, Jc, and Jared Henderson. 2019. "A Neglected Qua Solution to the Fundamental Problem of Christology." *Faith and Philosophy*. May 16, 2019. https://doi.org/10.5840/faithphil201957124.

Bird, Michael F., Dr. Craig A. Evans, Simon Gathercole, Charles E. Hill, and Chris Tilling. 2014. *How God Became Jesus: The Real Origins of Belief in Jesus' Divine Nature: A Response to Bart D. Ehrman*. 1st edition. Grand Rapids, MI: Zondervan Academic.

Bohn, Einar Duenger. 2012. "The Logic of the Incarnation." In *Logic in Orthodox Christian Thinking*, edited by Andrew Schumann, 104–121. Lancaster, UK: Gazelle Distribution.

Bonting, Sjoerd L. 2003. "Theological Implications of Possible Extraterrestrial Life." *Zygon* 38 (3): 587–602. https://doi.org/10.1111/1467–9744.00523.

Brazier, Paul. 2013. "C. S. Lewis: The Question of Multiple Incarnations." *Heythrop Journal* 55: 391–408. https://doi.org/10.1111/heyj.12049.

Brown, Christopher M. 2015. "Making the Best Even Better: Modifying Pawl and Timpe's Solution to the Problem of Heavenly Freedom." *Faith and Philosophy* 32 (1): 63–80.

Brümmer, Vincent. 1984. "Divine Impeccability." *Religious Studies* 20 (2): 203–214. https://doi.org/10.2307/20006044.

Canham, Michael McGhee. 2000. "Potuit Non Peccare Or Non Potuit Peccare: Evangelicals, Hermeneutics, and the Impeccability Debate." *The Masters Seminary Journal* 11 (1): 93–114

Carlson, John W. 2012. *Words of Wisdom: A Philosophical Dictionary for the Perennial Tradition.* 1st edition. South Bend, IN: University of Notre Dame Press.

Carter, W. R. 1985. "Impeccability Revisited." *Analysis* 45 (1): 52–55. https://doi.org/10.2307/3327405.

Cobreros, Pablo. 2016. "Supervaluationism and the Timeless Solution to the Foreknowledge Problem." *Scientia et Fides* 4 (1): 61–75.

Conn, Christopher Hughes. 2012. "Relative Identity, Singular Reference, and the Incarnation: A Response to Le Poidevin." *Religious Studies* 48 (01): 61–82. https://doi.org/10.1017/S0034412511000035.

Couehoven, Jesse. 2012. "The Necessities of Perfected Freedom." *International Journal of Systematic Theology* 14 (4): 396–419.

Cowan, Steven B. 2011. "Compatibilism and the Sinlessness of the Redeemed in Heaven." *Faith and Philosophy* 28 (4): 416–431.

Craig, William Lane. 2006. "Flint's Radical Molinist Christology Not Radical Enough." *Faith and Philosophy: Journal of the Society of Christian Philosophers* 23 (1): 55–64.

2018. *The Atonement.* Cambri: Cambridge University Press.

Crisp, Oliver D. 2004. "Did Christ Have a Fallen Human Nature?" *International Journal of Systematic Theology* 6 (3): 270–88.

2007a. "William Shedd on Christ's Impeccability." *Philosophia Christi* 9 (1): 165–188.

2007b. *Divinity and Humanity: The Incarnation Reconsidered.* 1st edition. Cambridge: Cambridge University Press.

2007c. "Was Christ Sinless or Impeccable?" *Irish Theological Quarterly* 72 (2): 168–186. https://doi.org/10.1177/0021140007082165.

2008. "Multiple Incarnations." In *Reason, Faith and History: Philosophical Essays for Paul Helm*, edited by Martin Stone, 219–238. Burlington, VT: Ashgate.

2009. *God Incarnate: Explorations in Christology.* 1st edition. New York: T&T Clark.

2011. "Compositional Christology without Nestorianism." In *The Metaphysics of the Incarnation*, edited by Anna Marmodoro and Jonathan Hill, 45–66. Oxford: Oxford University Press, USA.

2016. *The Word Enfleshed: Exploring the Person and Work of Christ*. Grand Rapids, MI: Baker Academic.

Cross, Richard. 2005. *The Metaphysics of the Incarnation: Thomas Aquinas to Duns Scotus*. Oxford: Oxford University Press.

2011. "The Incarnation." In *The Oxford Handbook of Philosophical Theology*, edited by Thomas P. Flint and Michael Rea, 452–475. Oxford: Oxford University Press.

2019. *Communicatio Idiomatum: Reformation Christological Debates*. Oxford: Oxford University Press.

Cuff, Andrew Jacob. 2015. "Duns Scotus and Jacques de Thérines on Free Will and the Word's Assumption of Human Nature." *Philosophy and Theology* 27 (2): 351–389.

Cupitt, Don. 1977. "The Christ of Christendom." In *The Myth of God Incarnate*, edited by John Hick, 133–147. Philadelphia, PA: Westminster Press.

Dahms, John V. 1978. "How Reliable Is Logic?" *Journal of the Evangelical Theological Society* 21 (4): 369–380.

Dalmau, Joseph. 2016. *On the One and Triune God*. Translated by Kenneth Baker. Vol. IIA. Sacrae Theologiae Summa IIA. Saddle River, NJ: Keep the Faith.

Davidson, Ivor J. 2008. "Pondering the Sinlessness of Jesus Christ: Moral Christologies and the Witness of Scripture." *International Journal of Systematic Theology* 10 (4): 372–398. https://doi.org/10.1111/j.1468-2400.2007.00331.x.

Davies, Brian. 2004. *An Introduction to the Philosophy of Religion*. 3rd edition. Oxford: Oxford University Press.

Davies, Paul. 2003. "ET and God." *Atlantic Monthly* 292 (2): 112–118.

Davis, Stephen T. 2006. "Is Kenosis Orthodox?" In *Exploring Kenotic Christology*, edited by C. Stephen Evans, 112–138. Oxford: Oxford University Press.

2011. "The Metaphysics of Kenosis." In *The Metaphysics of the Incarnation*, edited by Anna Marmodoro and Jonathan Hill, 114–133. Oxford: Oxford University Press.

Dawson, Samuel. 2004. "Is There a Contradiction in the Person of Christ? The Importance of the Dual Nature and Dual Consciousness of Jesus Christ." *Detroit Baptist Seminary Journal* 9: 161–181.

Deng, Natalja. 2018. *God and Time*. Cambridge: Cambridge University Press.

Denzinger, Henry. 2002. *The Sources of Catholic Dogma*. Fitzwilliam, NH: Loreto.

Deweese, Garrett. 2007. "One Person, Two Natures: Two Metaphysical Models of the Incarnation." In *Jesus in Trinitiarian Perspective*, edited by Fred Sanders and Klaus Issler, 114–153. Nashville, TN: B&H.

Dorner, Isaak August. 1994. *Divine Immutability: A Critical Reconsideration*. 1st edition. Minneapolis, MN: Fortress Press.

Dubray, Charles. 1911. "Nature." In *The Catholic Encyclopedia*. Vol. 10. New York: Robert Appleton Company. www.newadvent.org/cathen/10715a.htm.

Ehrman, Bart D. 2013. *Did Jesus Exist? The Historical Argument for Jesus of Nazareth*. New York: HarperOne.

Erickson, Millard J. 1996. *The Word Became Flesh: A Contemporary Incarnational Christology*. MIGrand Rapids,: Baker Academic.

Evans, C. Stephen. 2006a. *Exploring Kenotic Christology: The Self-Emptying of God*. Oxford: Oxford University Press.

 2006b. "Kenotic Christology and the Nature of God." In *Exploring Kenotic Christology*, edited by C. Stephen Evans, 190–217. Oxford: Oxford University Press.

Feenstra, Ronald. 1989. "Reconsidering Kenotic Christology." In *Trinity, Incarnation and Atonement*, edited by Ronald Feenstra and Cornelius Plantinga, 128–152. Notre Dame, IN: University of Notre Dame Press.

 2006. "A Kenotic Christology of Divine Attributes." In *Exploring Kenotic Christology*, edited by C. Stephen Evans, 139–164. Oxford: Oxford University Press.

Ferrier, Francis. 1962. *What Is the Incarnation?* 1st edition. New York: Hawthorn Books.

Fisher, Christopher L., and David Fergusson. 2006. "Karl Rahner and The Extra-Terrestrial Intelligence Question." *Heythrop Journal* 47 (2): 275–290.

Fisk, Philip J. 2007. "Jonathan Edwards's Freedom of the Will and His Defence of the Impeccability of Jesus Christ." *Scottish Journal of Theology* 60 (03): 309–325. https://doi.org/10.1017/S0036930607003304.

Flint, Thomas P. 2001. "The Possibilities of Incarnation: Some Radical Molinist Suggestions." *Religious Studies* 37 (3): 307–320.

 2011. "Should Concretists Part with Mereological Models of the Incarnation?" In *The Metaphysics of the Incarnation*, edited by Anna Marmodoro and Jonathan Hill, 67–87. Oxford: Oxford University Press.

2012. "Molinism and Incarnation." In *Molinism: The Contemporary Debate*, edited by Ken Perszyk, 187–207. Oxford: Oxford University Press.

2015. "Is Model T Rattle-Free?" *Faith and Philosophy* 32 (2): 177–181.

Forrest, Peter. 2009. "The Incarnation: A Philosophical Case for Kenosis." In *Oxford Readings in Philosophical Theology*, edited by Michael C. Rea, 225–238. Oxford: Oxford University Press.

Freddoso, Alfred. 1983. "Logic, Ontology and Ockham's Christology." *New Scholasticism* 57 (3): 293–330.

1986. "Human Nature, Potency and the Incarnation." *Faith and Philosophy* 3 (1): 27–53.

Funkhouser, Eric. 2006. "On Privileging God's Moral Goodness." *Faith and Philosophy* 23 (4): 409–422.

Gaine, Simon Francis. 2015a. "Christ's Acquired Knowledge According to Thomas Aquinas: How Aquinas's Philosophy Helped and Hindered His Account." *New Blackfriars* 96 (1063): 255–268.

2015b. *Did the Saviour See the Father?* London; Bloomsbury T&T Clark.

Garcia, Laura L. 1987. "The Essential Moral Perfection of God." *Religious Studies* 23 (1): 137–144.

Geddes, Leonard. 1911. "Person." In *The Catholic Encyclopedia*. Vol. 11. New York: Robert Appleton. www.newadvent.org/cathen/11726a.htm.

Gellman, Jerome. 1977. "Omnipotence and Impeccability." *New Scholasticism* 51 (December): 21–37.

George, Marie I. 2001. "Aquinas on Intelligent Extra-Terrestrial Life." *The Thomist* 65 (2): 239–258.

Gondreau, Paul. 2009. "St. Thomas Aquinas, the Communication of Idioms, and the Suffering of Christ in the Garden of Gethsemane." In *Divine Impassibility and the Mystery of Human Suffering*, edited by James F. Keating and Thomas Joseph White O.P. , 214–245. Grand Rapids, MI: Eerdmans.

2018. *The Passions of Christ's Soul in the Theology of St. Thomas Aquinas.* Cluny Media.

Gordon, James R. 2016. *The Holy One in Our Midst: An Essay on the Flesh of Christ.* Minneapolis, MN: Fortress Press.

Gorman, Michael. 2000a. "Personal Unity and the Problem of Christ's Knowledge." *Proceedings of the American Catholic Philosophical Association* 74: 175–186.

2000b. "Uses of the Person-Nature Distinction in Thomas's Christology." *Recherches de Theologie et Philosophie Medievales* 67 (1): 58–79.

2011. "Incarnation." In *The Oxford Handbook of Aquinas*, edited by Brian Davies and Eleonore Stump, 428–435. Oxford: Oxford University Press.

2014. "Christological Consistency and the Reduplicative Qua." *Journal of Analytic Theology* 2 (1): 86–100. https://doi.org/10.12978/jat.2014–1 .120811061413a.

2016. "Classical Theism, Classical Anthropology, and the Christological Coherence Problem." *Faith and Philosophy* 33 (3): 278–292. https://doi .org/10.5840/faithphil201662164.

2017. *Aquinas on the Metaphysics of the Hypostatic Union.* Cambridge: Cambridge University Press.

Green, Adam. 2017. "Omnisubjectivity and Incarnation." *Topoi* 36 (4): 693–701.

Harris, Kevin, and William Lane Craig. n.d. "Does Dr. Craig Have an Orthodox Christology?" Reasonable Faith. www.reasonablefaith.org/media/reason able-faith-podcast/does-dr.-craig-have-an-orthodox-christology.

Hart, Trevor A. 1995. "Sinlessness and Moral Responsibility: A Problem in Christology." *Scottish Journal of Theology* 48 (01): 37–54.

Hasker, William. 1998. *God, Time, and Knowledge.* Ithaca, NY: Cornell Univ Press.

2015. "Getting That Model T Back On the Road." *Faith and Philosophy* 32 (2): 172–176.

2016. "A Compositional Incarnation." Religious Studies. December 2016.

2017. *Incarnation: The Avatar Model.* Oxford: Oxford University Press. www.oxfordscholarship.com/view/10.1093/oso/9780198806967.001 .0001/oso-9780198806967-chapter-6.

2019. "The One Divine Nature." *TheoLogica: An International Journal for Philosophy of Religion and Philosophical Theology* 3 (2). https://doi.org /10.14428/thl.v3i1.2893.

Hebblethwaite, Brian. 2001. "The Impossibility of Multiple Incarnations." *Theology* 104 (821): 323–334. https://doi.org/10.1177/0040571X 0110400502.

2008. *Philosophical Theology and Christian Doctrine.* Oxford: Wiley.

Henderson, Luke. 2014. "Character-Development and Heaven." *International Journal for Philosophy of Religion* 76 (3): 319–330.

2016. "Impeccability and Perfect Virtue." *Religious Studies*, September, 1–20. https://doi.org/10.1017/S003441251600024X.

Hick, John. 1977. *The Myth of God Incarnate*. Louisville,KY: Westminster Press.

1989. "The Logic of God Incarnate." *Religious Studies* 25 (4): 409–423.

2006. *The Metaphor of God Incarnate, Second Edition: Christology in a Pluralistic Age*. Louisville, KY: Westminster John Knox Press.

Hill, Jonathan. 2012. "Incarnation, Timelessness, and Exaltation." *Faith and Philosophy* 29 (1): 3–29.

Hipp, Stephen. 2001. *"Person" in Christian Tradition and in the Conception of Saint Albert the Great*. Münster: Aschendorff.

Hofmann, Wilhelm, Roy F. Baumeister, Georg Förster, and Kathleen D. Vohs. 2012. "Everyday Temptations: An Experience Sampling Study of Desire, Conflict, and Self-Control." *Journal of Personality and Social Psychology* 102 (6): 1318–1335. https://doi.org/10.1037/a0026545.

Holland, Richard A. 2012. *God, Time, and the Incarnation*. Eugene,OR: Wipf & Stock.

Jaeger, Andrew. 2017. "Hylemorphic Animalism and the Incarnational Problem of Identity." *Journal of Analytic Theology* 5 (1): 145–162.

Jaeger, Andrew J., and Jeremy Sienkiewicz. 2018. "Matter without Form: The Ontological Status of Christ's Dead Body." *Journal of Analytic Theology* 6 (1): 131–145.

Jedwab, Joseph. 2011. "The Incarnation and Unity of Consciousness." In *The Metaphysics of the Incarnation*, edited by Anna Marmodoro and Jonathan Hill, 168–185. Oxford: Oxford University Press.

2015. "Against the Geachian Theory of the Trinity and Incarnation." *Faith and Philosophy* 32 (2): 125–145.

2018. "Timothy Pawl. In Defense of Conciliar Christology." *Journal of Analytic Theology* 6 (1): 743–747.

John of Damascus. 1958. *Fathers of the Church: Saint John of Damascus : Writings*. Translated by Frederic Chase. Washington, DC: Catholic University of America Press.

. 2000. *Saint John of Damascus: Writings*. Translated by Frederic Chase. Washington, DC: Catholic University of Amer Press.

Kavanagh, David J., Jackie Andrade, and Jon May. 2005. "Imaginary Relish and Exquisite Torture: The Elaborated Intrusion Theory of Desire." *Psychological Review* 112 (2): 446–467. https://doi.org/10.1037/0033-295X.112.2.446.

Kelly, Charles J. 1994. "The God of Classical Theism and the Doctrine of the Incarnation." *International Journal for Philosophy of Religion* 35 (1): 1–20.

Kereszty, Roch A. 2002. *Jesus Christ: Fundamentals of Christology*. Revised and updated 3rd Eedition. Staten Island, NY: Alba House.

Kevern, Peter. 2002. "Limping Principles: A Reply to Brian Hebblethwaite on 'The Impossibility of Multiple Incarnations.'" *Theology* 105 (827): 342–347. https://doi.org/10.1177/0040571X0210500503.

King, Rolfe. 2015. "Atonement and the Completed Perfection of Human Nature." *International Journal of Philosophy and Theology* 76 (1): 69–84. https://doi.org/10.1080/21692327.2015.1043931.

Klima, Gyula. 1984. "Libellus Pro Sapiente." *New Scholasticism* 58 (2): 207–219.

Labooy, G. H. 2019. "Stepped Characterisation: A Metaphysical Defence of qua-Propositions in Christology." *International Journal for Philosophy of Religion*, January. https://doi.org/10.1007/s11153-019-09698-y.

Le Poidevin, Robin. 2009a. "Identity and the Composite Christ: An Incarnational Dilemma." *Religious Studies* 45 (2): 167–186.

2009b. "Incarnation: Metaphysical Issues." *Philosophy Compass* 4 (4): 703–714.

2011. "Multiple Incarnations and Distributed Persons." In *The Metaphysics of the Incarnation*, edited by Anna Marmodoro and Jonathan Hill, 228–241. Oxford: Oxford University Press.

2013. "Kenosis, Necessity and Incarnation." *Heythrop Journal* 54 (2): 214–227. https://doi.org/10.1111/j.1468–2265.2012.00796.x.

Leftow, Brian. 1989. "Necessary Moral Perfection." *Pacific Philosophical Quarterly* 70 (3): 240–260.

1991. "Timelessness and Foreknowledge." *Philosophical Studies: An International Journal for Philosophy in the Analytic Tradition* 63 (3): 309–325.

2004. "A Timeless God Incarnate." In *The Incarnation*, edited by Stephen T. Davis, Daniel Kendall, and Gerald O'Collins, 273–299. Oxford: Oxford University Press.

2009. *Time and Eternity*. Ithaca, NY: Cornell University Press.

2011. "Composition and Christology." *Faith and Philosophy* 28 (3): 310–322.

2015. "Against Materialist Christology." In *Christian Philosophy of Religion: Essays in Honor of Stephen T. Davis*, edited by C. P. Ruloff, 65–94. Notre Dame, IN: University of Notre Dame Press.

Lim, Joungbin. 2019. "In Defense of Physicalist Christology." *Sophia*, June. https://doi.org/10.1007/s11841-019–0718-5.

Loke, Andrew. 2009. "On the Coherence of the Incarnation: The Divine Preconscious Model." *Neue Zeitschrift Für Systematische Theologie Und Religionsphilosophie* 51 (1): 50–63.

2011. "Solving a Paradox against Concrete-Composite Christology: A Modified Hylomorphic Proposal." *Religious Studies* 47 (4): 493–502. https://doi.org/10.1017/S0034412510000521.

2013. "The Incarnation and Jesus' Apparent Limitation in Knowledge." *New Blackfriars* 94 (1053): 583–602. https://doi.org/10.1111/j.1741–2005 .2012.01500.x.

2019. *The Origin of Divine Christology.* Reprint edition. Cambridge: Cambridge University Press.

Lonergan, Bernard. 2016. *The Incarnate Word: Volume 8.* Edited by Robert Doran, SJ, and Jeremy Wilkins. Translated by Charles Hefling Jr. 1st edition. Toronto: University of Toronto Press.

Luther, Martin. 1971. *Luther's Works: Word and Sacrament, 4.* Edited by Helmut T. Lehmann. Minneapolis, MN: Fortress Press.

Macquarrie, John. 1990. *Jesus Christ in Modern Thought.* 1st edition. London : SCM Press.

de Margerie, Bertrand. 1980. *Human Knowledge of Christ: The Knowledge, Fore-Knowledge and Consciousness, Even in the Pre-Paschal Period, of Christ the Redeemer.* Boston: Pauline Books and Media.

Maritain, Jacques. 1969. *On the Grace and Humanity of Jesus.* Translated by Joseph W. Evans. 1st edition. St. Louis, MO: Herder and Herder.

Marmodoro, Anna, and Jonathan Hill. 2008. "Modeling the Metaphysics of the Incarnation." *Philosophy and Theology.* July 1, 2008. https://doi.org/10 .5840/philtheol2008201/25.

2011. *The Metaphysics of the Incarnation.* Oxford: Oxford University Press.

Mascall, Eric Lionel. 1965. *Christian Theology and Natural Science: Some Questions in Their Relations.* Hamden, CT: Archon Books.

Mawson, T. J. 2018. *The Divine Attributes.* Cambridge: Cambridge University Press.

McCall, Thomas H. 2019. *Against God and Nature: The Doctrine of Sin.* Wheaton, IL: Crossway.

McDaniel, Kris. 2017. *The Fragmentation of Being.* Oxford: Oxford University Press.

McFarland, Ian. 2007. "'Willing Is Not Choosing': Some Anthropological Implications of Dyothelite Christology." *International Journal of Systematic Theology* 9 (1): 3–23.

2008. "Fallen or Unfallen? Christ's Human Nature and the Ontology of Human Sinfulness." *International Journal of Systematic Theology* 10 (4): 399–415. https://doi.org/10.1111/j.1468–2400.2008.00382.x.

McGinnis, Andrew M. 2014. *The Son of God beyond the Flesh: A Historical and Theological Study of the Extra Calvinisticum.* Bloomsbury.

McKinley, John Elton. 2009. *Tempted for Us: Theological Models and the Practical Relevance of Christ's Impeccability and Temptation*. Eugene, OR: Paternoster.

2011. "Four Patristic Models of Jesus Christ's Impeccability and Temptation." *Perichoresis* 9 (1): 29–66.

2015. "A Model of Jesus Christ's Two Wills in View of Theology Proper and Anthropology." *Southern Baptist Journal of Theology* 19 (1): 69–89.

McNabb, Tyler Dalton. 2018. *Religious Epistemology*. Cambridge: Cambridge University Press.

Merricks, Trenton. 2007. "The Word Made Flesh: Dualism, Physicalism, and the Incarnation." In *Persons: Human and Divine*, edited by Peter van Inwagen and Dean Zimmerman, 281–301. Oxford: Oxford University Press.

Milyavskaya, Marina, Michael Inzlicht, Nora Hope, and Richard Koestner. 2015. "Saying 'No' to Temptation: Want-to Motivation Improves Self-Regulation by Reducing Temptation Rather than by Increasing Self-Control." *Journal of Personality and Social Psychology* 109 (4): 677–693. https://doi.org/10.1037/pspp0000045.

Moloney, Raymond. 2000. *Knowledge of Christ*. 1st edition. London; Bloomsbury Academic.

Moreland, J. P., and William Lane Craig. 2003. *Philosophical Foundations for a Christian Worldview*. Downers Grove, IL: IVP Academic.

Morris, Thomas V. 1983. "Impeccability." *Analysis* 43 (2): 106–112.

1986. "Perfection and Power." *International Journal for Philosophy of Religion* 20 (2/3): 165–168.

1987. *The Logic of God Incarnate*. Ithaca, NY: Cornell University Press.

2009. "The Metaphysics of God Incarnate." In *Oxford Readings in Philosophical Theology*, edited by Michael C. Rea and Thomas P. Flint, 211–224. Oxford: Oxford University Press.

Mullins, R. T. 2016. *The End of the Timeless God*. Oxford: Oxford University Press.

Murray, Michael, and Michael C. Rea. 2008. *An Introduction to the Philosophy of Religion*. 1st edition. Cambridge: Cambridge University Press.

Nevitt, Turner C. 2016. "Aquinas on the Death of Christ." *American Catholic Philosophical Quarterly* 90 (1): 77–99.

O'Collins, Gerald. 1995. *Christology: A Biblical, Historical, and Systematic Study of Jesus Christ*. Oxford: Oxford University Press.

2002. "The Incarnation: The Critical Issues." In *The Incarnation*, edited by Stephen T. Davis, Daniel Kendall, and Gerald O'Collins, 1–30. Oxford: Oxford University Press.

Oord, Thomas Jay, William Hasker, and Dean Zimmerman. 2011. *God in an Open Universe: Science, Metaphysics, and Open Theism.* Eugene,OR: Pickwick.

Page, Ben. 2019. "Wherein Lies the Debate? Concerning Whether God Is a Person." *International Journal for Philosophy of Religion* 85 (3): 297–317. https://doi.org/10.1007/s11153-018-9694-x.

Pawl, Timothy. 2012. "Transubstantiation, Tropes and Truthmakers." *American Catholic Philosophical Quarterly* 86 (1): 71–96.

2014a. "A Solution to the Fundamental Philosophical Problem of Christology." *Journal of Analytic Theology* 2: 61–85.

2014b. "The Freedom of Christ and Explanatory Priority." *Religious Studies* 50 (2): 157–173. https://doi.org/10.1017/S0034412513000309.

2014c. "The Freedom of Christ and the Problem of Deliberation." *International Journal for Philosophy of Religion* 75 (3): 233–247.

2015. "Conciliar Christology and the Problem of Incompatible Predications." *Scientia et Fides* 3 (2): 85–106.

2016a. "Brian Hebblethwaite's Arguments against Multiple Incarnations." *Religious Studies* 52 (1): 117–130. https://doi.org/10.1017/S00344125 14000626.

2016b. "Temporary Intrinsics and Christological Predication." In *Oxford Studies in Philosophy of Religion, Volume 7*, edited by Jonathan L Kvanvig, 157–189. Oxford: Oxford University Press.

2016c. "Thomistic Multiple Incarnations." *Heythrop Journal* 57 (2): 359–370. https://doi.org/10.1111/heyj.12230.

2016d. *In Defense of Conciliar Christology: A Philosophical Essay.* 1st edition. Oxford: Oxford University Press.

2018. "Conciliar Christology and the Consistency of Divine Immutability with a Mutable, Incarnate God." *Nova et Vetera* 16 (3): 913–937.

2019a. "Explosive Theology: A Reply to Jc Beall's 'Christ – A Contradiction.'" *Journal of Analytic Theology* 7: 440–451.

2019b. *In Defense of Extended Conciliar Christology: A Philosophical Essay.* Oxford: Oxford University Press.

2020. "The Metaphysics of the Incarnation: Christ's Human Nature." In *Herausforderungen Und Modifikationen Des Klassischen Theismus*, edited by Thomas Marschler and Thomas Schärtl, forthcoming. Munster: Aschendorff.

Pawl, Timothy, and Mark Spencer. 2016. "Christologically Inspired, Empirically Motivated Hylomorphism." *Res Philosophica* 91 (1): 137–160.

Pawl, Timothy, and Kevin Timpe. 2009. "Incompatibilism, Sin, and Free Will in Heaven." *Faith and Philosophy* 26 (4): 398–419.

2013. "Heavenly Freedom: A Response to Cowan." *Faith and Philosophy* 30 (2): 188–197.

2016. "Freedom and the Incarnation." *Philosophy Compass* 11 (11): 743–756.

2017. "Paradise and Growing in Virtue." In *Paradise Understood*, 97–109. Oxford: Oxford University Press.

Pelser, Adam. 2019. "Temptation, Virtue, and the Character of Christ." *Faith and Philosophy: Journal of the Society of Christian Philosophers* 36 (1). https://place.asburyseminary.edu/faithandphilosophy/vol36/iss1/5.

Plantinga, Alvin. 1999. "On Heresy, Mind, and Truth." *Faith and Philosophy* 16 (2): 182–193.

Pohle, Joseph. 1911. *The Divine Trinity: A Dogmatic Treatise*. St. Louis, MO: B. Herder.

1913. *Christology: A Dogmatic Treatise on the Incarnation*. St. Louis, MO: B. Herder.

Rea, Michael. 2011. "Hylomorphism and the Incarnation." In *The Metaphysics of the Incarnation*, edited by Anna Marmodoro and Jonathan Hill, 134–152. Oxford: Oxford University Press.

Rea, Michael C. 2003. "Relative Identity and the Doctrine of the Trinity." *Philosophia Christi* 5 (2): 431–445. https://doi.org/10.5840/pc20035247.

Rebenich, Stefan. 2002. *Jerome*. London; Routledge.

Rhoda, Alan. 2007. "The Philosophical Case for Open Theism." *Philosophia* 35 (3–4): 301–311.

2008. "Generic Open Theism and Some Varieties Thereof." *Religious Studies* 44 (2): 225–234.

2011. "The Fivefold Openness of the Future." In *God in an Open Universe*, edited by William Hasker, Thomas Jay Oord, and Dean Zimmerman, 69–93. Eugene, OR: Pickwick.

Riches, Aaron. 2016. *Ecce Homo: On the Divine Unity of Christ*. Grand Rapids, MI: Eerdmans.

Rogers, Katherin A. 2010. "Incarnation." In *The Cambridge Companion to Christian Philosophical Theology*, edited by Charles Taliaferro and Chad V. Meister, 95–107. Cambridge: Cambridge University Press.

2013. "The Incarnation As Action Composite." *Faith and Philosophy*. August 1, 2013. https://doi.org/10.5840/faithphil201330324.

2016. "Christ's Freedom: Anselm vs Molina." *Religious Studies* FirstView (July): 1–16. https://doi.org/10.1017/S0034412516000093.

Rosenberg, Randall S. 2010. "Christ's Human Knowledge: A Conversation with Lonergan and Balthasar." *Theological Studies* 71 (4): 817–845. https://doi.org/10.1177/004056391007100403.

Rota, Michael. 2010. "The Eternity Solution to the Problem of Human Freedom and Divine Foreknowledge." *European Journal for Philosophy of Religion* 2 (1): 165–186.

Sanders, John. 1998. *The God Who Risks: A Theology of Providence*. Downers Grove, IL: InterVarsity Press.

Scarpelli, Therese. 2007. "Bonaventure's Christocentric Epistemology: Christ's Human Knowledge As the Epitome of Illumination in De Scientia Christi." *Franciscan Studies* 65 (1): 63–86.

Schmaus, Michael. 1971. *Dogma 3: God and His Christ*. 1st edition. Mission, KS: Sheed and Ward.

Senor, Thomas D. 2002. "Incarnation, Timelessness, and Leibniz's Law Problems." In *God and Time: Essays on the Divine Nature*, edited by Gregory E. Ganssle and David M. Woodruff, 220–235. Oxford: Oxford University Press.

2011. "Drawing on Many Traditions: An Ecumenical Kenotic Christology." In *The Metaphysics of the Incarnation*, edited by Anna Marmodoro and Jonathan Hill, 88–113. Oxford: Oxford University Press.

Sharpe, Kevin W. 2017. "The Incarnation, Soul-Free: Physicalism, Kind Membership, and the Incarnation." *Religious Studies* 53 (1): 117–131. https://doi.org/10.1017/S0034412515000530.

Sollier, Joseph. 1907. "Apollinarianism." In *The Catholic Encyclopedia*. New York: Robert Appleton. www.newadvent.org/cathen/01615b.htm.

Spence, Alan. 2008. *Christology: A Guide for the Perplexed*. London; T & T Clark.

Stump, Eleonore. 1989. "Review of Morris' The Logic of God Incarnate." *Faith and Philosophy* 6: 218–223.

1999. "Orthodoxy and Heresy." *Faith and Philosophy* 16 (2): 147–163. https://doi.org/10.5840/faithphil199916217.

2004. "Aquinas's Metaphysics of the Incarnation." In *The Incarnation*, edited by Stephen T. Davis, Daniel Kendall, and Gerald O'Collins, 197–218. Oxford: Oxford University Press.

2005. *Aquinas*. New York: Routledge.

2019. *Atonement*. Oxford: Oxford University Press.

Stump, Eleonore, and Norman Kretzmann. 1981. "Eternity." *Journal of Philosophy* 78 (8): 429–458. https://doi.org/10.2307/2026047.

1991. "Prophecy, Past Truth, and Eternity." *Philosophical Perspectives* 5: 395–424. https://doi.org/10.2307/2214103.

Sturch, Richard. 1991. *The Word and the Christ: An Essay in Analytic Christology*. Oxford; Oxford University Press.

Swinburne, Richard. 1993. *The Coherence of Theism*. Revised edition. Oxford: Oxford University Press.

    1994. *The Christian God*. 1st edition. Oxford: Oxford University Press.

Tamburro, Richard. 2014. *The Free Actions of Glorified Saints*. York: University of York.

Tanner, Norman P. 1990. *Decrees of the Ecumenical Councils 2 Volume Set*. Washington, DC: Georgetown University Press.

    2001. *The Councils of the Church: A Short History*. New York: Crossroad.

Thompson, Thomas R. 2006. "Nineteenth-Century Kenotic Christology: The Waxing, Waning, and Weighing of a Quest for a Coherent Orthodoxy." In *Exploring Kenotic Christology*, edited by C. Stephen Evans, 74–111. Oxford: Oxford University Press.

Tilling, Chris. 2015. *Paul's Divine Christology*. Eerdmans.

Tuggy, Dale. 2007. "Three Roads to Open Theism." *Faith and Philosophy* 24 (1): 28–51.

Turcescu, Lucian. 2005. *Gregory of Nyssa and the Concept of Divine Persons*. New York: Oxford University Press.

Turner, James T. 2017. "On Two Reasons Christian Theologians Should Reject the Intermediate State." *Journal of Reformed Theology* 11 (1–2): 121–139. https://doi.org/10.1163/15697312–01101023.

    2019. "Hylemorphism, Rigid Designators, and the Disembodied 'Jesus': A Call for Clarification." *Religious Studies*, March, 1–16. https://doi.org/10.1017/S0034412519000040.

Twombly, Charles C. 2015. *Perichoresis and Personhood: God, Christ, and Salvation in John of Damascus*. Eugene, OR: Pickwick.

Vallicella, William F. 2002. "Incarnation and Identity." *Philo* 5 (1): 84–93.

Van Inwagen, Peter. 1998. "Incarnation and Christology." In *Routledge Encyclopedia of Philosophy*, edited by E. Craig. London: Routledge. www.rep.routledge.com/article/K038SECT4.

Van Horn, Luke. 2010. "Merricks's Soulless Savior." *Faith and Philosophy: Journal of the Society of Christian Philosophers* 27 (3): 330–341.

Ward, Keith. 1998. *God, Faith, and the New Millennium: Christian Belief in an Age of Science*. Oxford: Oneworld.

Ware, Bruce A. 2013. *The Man Christ Jesus: Theological Questions on the Humanity of Christ*. Wheaton, IL: Crossway.

Weinandy, Thomas G. 2004. "Jesus' Filial Vision of the Father." *Pro Ecclesia* 13 (2): 189–201.

    2014. *Jesus: Essays in Christology*. Ave Maria, FL: Catholic University of America Press.

Weis, E. A. 2003. "Impeccability of Christ." In *New Catholic Encyclopedia*, 2nd edition, 7:361. Detroit, MI: Gale.

Wellum, Stephen J. 2016. *God the Son Incarnate: The Doctrine of Christ*. WheatonIL: Crossway.

Wesche, Kenneth Paul. 1997. *On the Person of Christ: The Christology of Emperor Justinian*. Crestwood, N.Y: St Vladimirs Seminary Press.

Werther, David. 1993. "The Temptation of God Incarnate." *Religious Studies* 29 (1): 47–50. https://doi.org/10.2307/20019589.

 2005. "Divine Foreknowledge, Harry Frankfurt, and 'Hyper-Incompatibilism.'" *Ars Disputandi* 5 (1): 79–85. https://doi.org/10.1080/15665399.2005.10819868.

 2012. "Freedom, Temptation, and Incarnation." In *Philosophy and the Christian Worldview: Analysis, Assessment and Development*, edited by David Werther and Mark Linville, 252–64. New York: Continuum.

Wessling, Jordan. 2013. "Christology and Conciliar Authority." In *Christology: Ancient & Modern*, edited by Oliver D. Crisp and Fred Sanders. Grand Rapids, MI: Zondervan.

White, Thomas Joseph. 2005. "The Voluntary Action of the Earthly Christ and the Necessity of the Beatific Vision." *The Thomist* 69 (4): 497–534.

 2016. *The Incarnate Lord: A Thomistic Study in Christology*. Washington, DC: Catholic University of America Press.

Williams, C. J. F. 1968. "A Programme for Christology." *Religious Studies* 3 (2): 513–524.

Willis, E. David. 1966. *Calvin's Catholic Christology: The Function of the So-Called Extra Calvinisticum in Calvin's Theology*. Brill.

Zagzebski, Linda Trinkaus. 1991. *The Dilemma of Freedom and Foreknowledge*. 1st edition. New York: Oxford University Press.

Acknowledgments

I thank those who participated in a workshop on the manuscript of this book at the Logos Institute for Analytic and Exegetical Theology (University of St Andrews): Dennis Bray, Joshua Cockayne, Preston Hill, Matthew Joss, Carol King, Derek King, Christa McKirland, Jonathan Rutledge, Andrew Torrance, and Koert Verhagen. I thank the Logos Institute for a senior research fellowship (2019), during which this book was written, and the Templeton Religious Trust (ID: TRT0095/58801) for funding that fellowship. I thank Jc Beall, Mark DelCogliano, David Efird – whose recent death is a tragic loss in so many ways – W. Matthews Grant, Hud Hudson, Noah Jones, Gavin Kerr, Ryan Mullins, Ben Page, Faith Pawl, Michael Rea, Mark Spencer, Jim Stone, Allison Timpe (but not Kevin Timpe), and Chandler Warren for comments on the manuscript. I thank the John Templeton Foundation for a grant (ID: 61012), which provided some of the research time I used in the writing of this book.

I thank Fr. George Welzbacher for reading the entire manuscript and giving careful comments in his official role as *Censor Librorum* for the Archdiocese of St. Paul and Minneapolis. I thank Fr. Welzbacher for providing a *Nihil Obstat* to the book, and Most Reverend Bernard A. Hebda, Archbishop of Saint Paul and Minneapolis, for his *Imprimatur*.

This book is dedicated to Faith Pawl, an excellent human. (The praise I intended to include here was brilliant, moving, and longer than word limits allow. Trust me: it was the sort of thing you dream of reading about yourself, and not a bit of it was undeserved.)

Cambridge Elements ≡

Philosophy of Religion

Yujin Nagasawa

University of Birmingham

Yujin Nagasawa is Professor of Philosophy and Co-director of the John Hick Centre for Philosophy of Religion at the University of Birmingham. He is currently President of the British Society for the Philosophy of Religion. He is a member of the editorial board of *Religious Studies*, the *International Journal for Philosophy of Religion* and *Philosophy Compass*.

About the Series

This Cambridge Elements series provides concise and structured introductions to all the central topics in the philosophy of religion. It offers balanced, comprehensive coverage of multiple perspectives in the philosophy of religion. Contributors to the series are cutting-edge researchers who approach central issues in the philosophy of religion. Each provides a reliable resource for academic readers and develops new ideas and arguments from a unique viewpoint.

Philosophy of Religion

Printed in the United States
By Bookmasters